REIMAGINED

BY

IAN BRECK

Reimagine life!

Ian Breck Publishing Group

An imprint of River Bend Research, Fishers, Indiana 46038

Visit us at IanBreck.com

REVISED SECOND EDITION

REIMAGINED™ Copyright © 2012 by River Bend Research, LLC. All rights reserved under International and Pan-American Copyright Conventions. By payment of the required fees, you have been granted the non-exclusive, non-transferable right to access and read the text of this e-book on-screen. No part of this text may be reproduced, transmitted, scanned, downloaded, decompiled, reverse engineered, or stored in or introduced into any information storage and retrieval system, in any form or by any means, whether electronic or mechanical, now known or hereinafter invented, without the express written permission of River Bend Research. "The Reimagined Life" is a trademark of River Bend Research, LLC. SECOND EDITION Library of Congress Cataloging-in-Publication Data has been applied for. Print Edition © March 2012.

Breck, Ian (2012-03-05). REIMAGINED River Bend Research, LLC.

ZR: 9500-2312-3432-120-66

Print Edition

ISBN: 978-0-9849123-2-2

10 9 8 7 6 5 4 3 2

DEDICATION

So many people have made my work and this book possible. They've tolerated a researcher almost ruining their lives with late hours and emotions ranging from euphoria to dazed confusion and utter frustration. In case you've never experienced someone like me in your life, I'm told it's not that great. However, I just think they're angry because I've never been particularly good about remembering birthdays and holidays.

I would especially like to thank Sandy, whose constant inspiration, encouragement, and tolerance has made my career and this book possible.

The individual you can most blame for all of this is my father. I shall leave him nameless as to spare him the public humiliation of fathering of a son who finds his thrills in understanding how humans think, and how they use their knowledge to live their lives on an otherwise chaotic planet. However, he has been a good father despite myself. I'm thankful he's a part of my life.

Oh yes, many of the names in this book have been changed, or are composites of real people I have known throughout the years. If you think that's not cool, you've obviously never written about your colleagues, friends, acquaintances, and neighbors, and had to face them the day after your book is published.

To all of the rest who have made my life a nicer place to be - without whom naught. Thank you.

CONTENTS

PROLOGUE
ix

A LIFE UNREALIZED
1

IMAGINE
13

Section One: Life Lessons

BECOMING YOU
25

A RIDICULOUSLY SHORT COURSE IN KNOWLEDGE
37

THOSE BEAUTIFUL YOU'S
59

INTRODUCING MOZART
69

DECISIONS. DECISIONS.
85

LIFE QUALITIES
99

Section Two: Life Strategies

THE QUALITY LIFE
109

IT'S A YOU THING
115

UNIQUELY YOU
123

A LIFE OF PASSION
133

RELATIONSHIPS
141

INDEPENDENCE
155

KEEPING IT REAL
169

EXPECTING MORE
177

STANDING
189

LOVING DEEPLY
2197

THE LEARNED
207

LIFE'S CURRENCY
215

HOW IT ALL WORKS TOGETHER
227

Section Three: Life Design

PUTTING IT ALL TOGETHER
233

YOUR LIFE'S DESIGN
241

AFTERWORD
259

Reader Notes Pages
263-267

Publisher's Note...

This book contains novel research findings, illustrative discussions and models pertaining to life and living concepts designed to provide greater clarity. It's not designed, nor is it intended to diagnose, treat, or cure any illness or dysfunction, or serve as a substitute for professional assistance or guidance.

Please use appropriate discretion and common sense when making life changes. Remember that you always have the last word and final responsibility for the decisions that shape your life.

For more information or to ask questions, please visit us online at IanBreck.com.

viii | **Reimagined**

PROLOGUE

> *"If you want to live an amazing life, learn how it works – and then become creative with it!"*
>
> ~ **Ian Breck**

When I first became interested in how people with exceptional lives differed from the rest, my firm conducted a survey that posed one question to more than 43,000 people: "What is a *quality* life?" More than 99% of the respondents could not answer this question with any degree of clarity or confidence. Only a few years later, we discovered that fewer than 1% of all people will experience a life they actually "love."

This book explains why.

So, why do some people live exceptional lives, but the vast majority don't? If the good life isn't about money, fame, or the corner office, then what is it about? More importantly, are exceptional lives the domain of the privileged few, or something anyone can experience – and if so, how?

This book answers these questions - *and many more.*

As a cognitive design and life quality researcher for more than 25 years, I'm frequently asked questions like these. However, most people simply want to know if it's still possible to experience an exceptional life in a world that's lost its sense of direction. My answer is always the same, *"If you understand how life works well enough to become creative with it, life can always be amazing!"* Unfortunately, this is where most people stumble on their journey to the lives they dream of living. Life and how we design, live, and love it are things we're never taught.

This book corrects this.

So, what is happening with life today? There certainly is no scarcity of blame for our diminished quality of life. Unrelenting stress, anxiety, fear, uncertainty, career challenges, the economy, corruption, predatory business and government practices, and much more are inhibiting our ability to flourish. We've become so immersed in simply surviving, that happiness is one of those things we shuffle under our growing pile of things to do before we die. While all of these things burden life quality, they're not the reasons we're exceeding our design limits. The truth is that most people simply don't understand how life works, and are failing to design and live lives that keep up with their realities. We're failing to live the lives we dream of living. We're failing to thrive. We're failing to be happy.

This book breaks this chain.

A wonderful experience is one of life's most achievable tasks – provided you understand what you're doing, of course. A deeply satisfying and rewarding life isn't something you're born with and has nothing to do with power, money, fame, or provenance. Amazing lives are imagined, created, lived, nourished, and valued. Those with truly remarkable lives have greater understandings about life and living, and use their knowledge to design and live richer, more meaningful lives. The design of your life determines your overall experience. If your life design isn't exceeding your realities, discontentment is the canary in the coal mine telling you changes are in order. Luckily, an amazing life is always within your reach!

This book shows you how.

There's no reason to live a life you don't *love*. A new generation is drawing lines in the sand and saying, "enough is enough!" They're taking back the control of and responsibility for their own lives. They're reimagining, redesigning, and living their lives in unexpected and imaginative new ways. They're rediscovering the value, promise, and security that a life well lived provides, and are overwhelming life's toughest challenges through smarter life choices and intelligent life design. These are *High Q people* - and they have a great deal to teach about life and living.

This book introduces you to them.

I wrote this book for people of all ages wanting to understand more about life, living, and how it all works together to create a more amazing you. You'll be introduced to *reimagination*. Reimagination brings together knowledge about life and living with insights from those who already live quality lives and your desire to design and live a more amazing life. Whether your life could use only a few tweaks, or a complete overhaul, you'll learn far more about yourself, and walk away with an actionable blueprint for the next chapters of your life.

This book introduces you to creating and living a life around your passions and interests. It's intended to be used and not just read. We'll explore intriguing concepts and develop new understandings about living on your own terms. You'll also learn what makes High Q people unique, and what their uniqueness means to you. Furthermore, you'll discover new ways of thinking with the power to change your life and help you to rediscover the you that's been waiting to live a breathtaking life.

This book isn't about religion, nebulous methodologies, mysticism, the latest fads, or new age thinking. It's about rediscovering how you think, function, and live *naturally*. When combined with my unwavering belief that understanding life more completely allows you to become creative with it, there's nothing stopping you from living the life you've always dreamed about living!

Ultimately, this book is about *you*. It's about imagining and designing a life that's truly amazing at every age and level of accomplishment. It's living your passions and passionate living - and building a life around what's truly important and valuable to you. It's not just about living life - *it's about loving it!*

This book is the missing life manual we all wished we had long ago. It's designed for lawyers who secretly want to be chefs, students who dream of becoming astronauts, librarians who surreptitiously fantasize about being novelists - and anyone who wants to simply love life again. It's about you, your passions and dreams that are desperately seeking to become a part of an amazing life yet to be fully realized. This book is about your second, third, or perhaps even sixtieth chance to design and live your life on your own terms – and get it right.

You were designed to live an amazing life. Let's get started!

"Living a wonderful life starts with designing a life that's worth living."

~ **Ian Breck**

CHAPTER ONE
A LIFE UNREALIZED

"It's never too late to write a happy ending for your life."

~ **Ian Breck**

It was all so bright, yet blurry for some reason. The nebulous atmosphere was punctuated with incessant beeping and frenzied voices. It was cool – no, downright chilly. Everything smelled of alcohol and sterility. Beeps continued their unrelenting taunt as I tried to get back to sleep and escape this merciless nightmare. A cool hand tapped my wrist and gently shook my shoulder under an unfamiliar blanket. "Ian, wake up! Wake up! Hey, we removed about 4 feet of your intestines, part of your duodenum, and mesentery. It was cancer. I think we got it all. I'll see you tomorrow."

That was it! The message was as cool and sterile as the environment itself – even with the warm Britishesque South African accent of my brilliant, life-restoring surgeon. He and his team had just spent the last five or so hours disemboweling me in their pursuit of surreptitious tumors. They removed, examined, and replaced my intestines, liver, stomach, spleen, pancreas, stomach and other goodies that only physicians can enunciate and appreciate. Aside from the inevitable scarring of my body, it was my surgeon's remarks that had etched even deeper wounds in my psyche. As amazing a surgeon and person as he is, I can't help but remember wishing he'd simply let me die on the table. Actually, who would have known? Who would have cared? At least it would have been peaceful.

At that very moment, my life changed profoundly. Behind my glassy eyes was a shattered soul gasping for air. I remember hoping I might awaken to start my day like every other. No day would ever be as any other. I'd just become a statistic. I was scared and alone, despite the legion of people buzzing around me. Cancer was living inside of me and killing me one cell at a time. Cancer is a horrific journey of one and oneness. What it does to your mind is just as bad, if not worse, than what it does to your body.

Over the previous four years, I'd been immersed in figuring out how my business would survive an America raped by big banks, Wall Street firms, and a government that stood by silently as the world's greatest theft and fraud took place. The single greatest fleecing in the history of the world was under way and my clients were dropping like flies. Ninety-five percent of them are no longer in business. Yet, not one banker, executive, or politician has ever been prosecuted as an accessory to economic collapse; all walked away from any degree of culpability thanks to what the Feds call *systemic risk*. Discovering how to survive an economy destroyed by the greed and avarice of its own financial system, leaders, and an overtly obliging government had me mad as hell and questioning the American dream along with millions of others. Yet a tiny group of microscopic incurable cancer cells that occurs in fewer than 2 out of 100,000 people had rendered America's domestic terrorists irrelevant for the moment.

I never forgot my surgeon's words despite trying desperately to do so. They not only forever changed my life – they also changed how I look at life. Like most victims of cancer, I spent incalculable time and energy asking questions with no apparent answers. I firmly believe all physicians are required to take at least one course in ambiguity during medical school. It's a simple course, really. All questions are answered with phrases like, "We don't really know that" or, "I'm not sure." If they fail as physicians, their skills transfer perfectly to politics. My life was suddenly one of medical clichés, brick walls, and stairways to nowhere. Control of my life was no longer mine.

The emotional pain of losing control of your destiny is indescribable. I wanted a pill to make it all go away – or perhaps just to make me go away. I'll admit it - I thought about suicide for a brief moment in time. Life had suddenly become very different to me. None of my dreams and aspirations really meant anything anymore. The ones I had yet to achieve were suddenly gone. I had to start my so-called life over again with my new and uninvited reality. As it turned out, my biggest problem was I simply didn't know how to start over again. Despite being an expert about life issues, I'd never applied my own work to myself. Until that point, all of my expertise had been theoretical – and so had my life.

In my quest for answers, I stumbled upon the sobering fact that President Nixon's declared war on cancer in 1971 largely has been a failure. My gastroenterologist remarked that his most realistic hope was that someday cancer would become a chronic condition as opposed to a death sentence. Although we may be able to detect cancer earlier, once it sets up shop, our options remain extremely limited in all too many cases. I also became aware of the indiscriminate nature of cancer - it kills babies too. Cancer not only kills one of every two men and one of every three women; it's also a leading cause of childhood mortality. Cancer is something that happens to "other" people – at least until you become one of them yourself.

Those days were among the longest and most painful of my life. Time passed at a snail's pace – and too quickly. I often found myself behind the computer searching for answers and crumbs of hope at all hours of the day and night. Dr. Google offered good news, bad news, hope, fear, snake oil, misdirection, voodoo, and speculation. It was all there for the taking. I remember becoming so inundated that I would lie in bed and cry so hard I could barely breathe. I no longer had control of my life and had even lesser hope for it. One day my oncologist looked at the expression on my face and said, "Ian, you don't have to live like this. Let me set you up with a psychologist I know." I reminded him rather snappishly that neither Freud nor Jung were particularly successful at making one's demise any more palatable, convenient, or graceful.

Nevertheless, I thanked him for his recommendation and went on with my day.

What had begun only four years earlier as a question of how my company would survive a looted and raped America, had given way to exploring the best ways to spend my last years - or perhaps months, if that's all I had.

Weeks and months came and went. Time became the backdrop of serious philosophical and existential explorations of my life as well as my ideas about living it. I waded through my life only to expose a rather shallow one-dimensional existence despite many venerated accomplishments – and yet, it was so unlike the passion-filled life I had envisioned as a young man. Perhaps the most sobering of all of my insights was the realization my life had somehow defined me as opposed to me defining it. I did the big stuff; however, it's the small stuff that matters most. That's what happens when you live life day-to-day. Life fills the voids you miss - or are simply too busy to fill yourself.

After examining my life ad nauseum over the next months, everything I thought I knew came into question. As I sat in my hospital bed after a second abdominal surgery, I found myself once again reliving my professional victories, achievements, and accomplishments as I stared blankly through a window covered with drops of rain framing a dreary gray sky - and a world sputtering along blindly as if I never existed. I realized that if I died, nothing would really change. Meetings about upcoming meetings with the usual grandstanding subject lines would continue uninterrupted. Ineffectual managers, otherwise henpecked at home, would continue terrorizing employees afraid of losing their jobs in an effort to disguise their true incompetencies and spineless natures. Google would forget my name in only a few months. The paperboy would miss my front porch – again. Politicians would continue lying as they kissed little children and left doors open to clandestine trysts with lonely soccer moms begging for any semblance of attention – and, all as if I'd never existed.

So, did I really ever matter? Did all of my accomplishments really make a difference, or mean anything to anyone except me? Is this all there is to life? I understand that we all have to go sometime, but this sometime seemed particularly unreasonable. I wasn't done! In fact, I hadn't even started living yet! I was forty-whatever and had lived my life for everyone - *but me.* I was *next* on my list of life's to-do's!

Along with my frustration came the most difficult part of my new and uninvited reality - figuring out how to tell the ones I love so deeply, "good-bye," and "thank you for being with me on my journey and making my life a more extraordinary place to be." Words just aren't that profound – they're simply not designed for stuff that deep.

As sleepless nights and personal retrospectives continued, I entertained the unspeakable notion that perhaps my beliefs and perceptions about life had been wrong all along. I read somewhere that Freud disputed many of his own theories later in life. Why couldn't I do the same? Despite researching life for over two decades, the ultimate irony was that I'd never really taken the time to explore my own life within the context of my work. It's kind of like a carpenter's house always being the last one they work on. If I had the chance to do it all over again, I would do so many things very differently.

At that very moment, I became shamelessly and much more loudly indignant about the injustices brought about by the hubris and avarice of execrable people. I also became more appreciative of the good in my life I took for granted. Suddenly, life's true magnificence became clearer. Seeing life from six feet under is funny that way.

Years ago, I coined the phrase *"twilight clarity"* to describe the experience people have when they look back on their lives with almost perfect clarity in the months, weeks, days, and hours before they die. Mine had just begun. I saw life with a more delicate eye and motiveless appreciation. The dance, music and tempo of life and living suddenly became perfectly clear to me. The inexhaustible and addictive pulse of New York City, the verdant solace of the Berkshires, the deafening whispers of wind-caressed Kansas wheat fields, and the violently thunderous majesty of ocean waves crashing into the rocky shores of Half Moon Bay and Big Sur became profound and inspiring as opposed to merely beautiful. It was then I realized the greatest design flaw of humanity is how the fog of everyday living all too often masks the true beauty and amazement life presents.

For the first time I understood how George Bailey felt in *It's a Wonderful Life*. The only difference being I had no plans of ending it all. I wanted to live like never before and for as long as possible. I wanted a second go at it – but with what I know today. This time, however, I wanted to do it smarter, and *better*. This time I wanted to live and experience my life for me instead of everyone else. Life is just too damned short to live it for anyone else or by their standards. I still had things to do - and people to piss off!

That particular day I arrived home to a very welcoming Gizmo, my 6-month old Havanese puppy. He's also known as "Pup-O-Love," "Pup Dog," "Gizmert," "Doggers," "G-Dog," "Grand Master G" and "Pup Daddy G" - his badass rap names (every nine-pound dog needs at least one). I still laugh when Gizmo all but drills himself into the ground spinning, zipping, and running around in circles from his unbridled joy of seeing me. The thing I love most about Gizmo (and humans who do the same), is his unapologetic inability to feign excitement. I may not mean anything to the rest of the world, but to Gizmert, I'm a rock star! I picked him up and hugged him like never before as he licked my face with his extraordinary soul-nourishing dog spittle. I never much cared for dog slobber on my face, but on that day, it was the perfect period at the end of a very long and exhausting sentence. Gizmo hugged me back as best as he could for not having opposable thumbs. It was one of life's perfect moments. Nothing remotely compares to the love of my goofy little dog. Knowing that Gizmo missed and loved me so much meant everything to me at that moment. He gave me a reason to exist when I needed one most. Gizmo was exactly what I needed to realize my life did have value – if to no one else but him. That was good enough for me.

It's funny how the little things in life become so important and meaningful when we're alone with just our thoughts. However, those are the things and moments that define our lives and who we are. That night, Gizmo and I lay on the sofa together, ate popcorn, watched a movie, and drifted to sleep under the blanket. And we were happy.

A Better Mousetrap

Perhaps the supreme illogicality of life is that we become so immersed in living it, that it requires a life-altering event like disease, death, failure, a new baby, marriage, loss of a job, or other destabilizing occurrence before we realize life is out of balance or control. By time we recognize a life audit is necessary, our behaviors, beliefs, and patterns have become so deeply entangled and highly compiled that any reasonable hope for unraveling them has all but vanished. The results often include frustration, hopelessness, and despair as we confront our unrealized potential.

To add insult to injury, those events that trigger truly meaningful and contemplative life reevaluations rarely occur when we're most able to handle them – during our early years. Instead, life's grandest epiphanies tend to rear their ugly heads later in life when our bodies, minds, and courage are more brittle, and our fears of failure present almost insurmountable obstacles to our ultimate happiness. That's just how life rolls, I guess. There's not a "fairness" clause anywhere to be found. I've been looking for decades.

Regardless of reason or timing, the initial results of an evaluated life are often the same: the disconcerting realization that our days are numbered, we've wasted invaluable time, and there has to be more to life than what we've experienced to this point. It's a sobering realization that's also strangely motivating.

People respond to their realization that life is passing too quickly in any number of ways. Some seek to pack as much life into their remaining days as possible, as in *The Bucket List*. For others, it's all about slowing down, redefining life, and filling their lives with the enormous good the world has to offer - more like *Under the Tuscan Sun*. For some people, it's about small refinements to an already pretty good life. For others, it's about the exciting potential of walking away from the ordinary and creating a refreshing new chapter. Regardless of the degree of transformation desired, most never make it far because they simply don't understand how to change their lives.

Until my epiphany, my expertise about life and living had been reserved for corporations and governments. As an expert in life and knowledge structures, I enjoyed a worldwide audience. For the first time, however, I was being challenged by my own reality. Group behavior, corporations, and keynotes along with laughable and misleading notions like teamwork being even remotely possible, or that competition is usually good, no longer had a place in my new and less coddling vernacular. It was all about *me* this time. I possibly had a second chance that few do – and didn't know how long it would last. I'd spent my entire life understanding everyone else's life. Now it was time to learn more about my own. Doctor, heal thyself.

So, how does one reimagine their entire life? I realized quickly that it's not so much about wasting time and energy building a better mousetrap with all of the messy undoing and reshaping involved. It's more about creating a better mouse. It was time to create a better *me*.

I started only with the knowledge that a quality life isn't anything someone simply creates. It's a far more complex thing than that. A quality life requires an environment that nourishes it and enables it to thrive. If the environment isn't right or present, a quality life cannot exist. It's that simple. I know, it sounds peculiar right now, but never forget it. It's a core law of life and living that's carved in stone. I tell my clients a quality life is like a martini that exists only when gin, vermouth, and an olive or three are present in said stemmed Martini goblet. Remove any single ingredient, and you have something with the sex appeal of spaghetti at an autopsy. A quality life is precisely the same. When everything's in place, it's amazing. When not, it's, "Pass the pancreas, please!"

The recipe for an exceptional life starts with a basic life, and ends with generous splashes of exceptional ingredients added to taste. However, forget about what Madison Avenue wants you to think a quality life is. It's not about cars, perky boobs, luxurious perfume, money, perfect teeth, or a political office – you can buy those things. Nor is a quality life about mind-numbing twelve-step programs. There are no shortcuts to living an amazing life; you have one or you don't. You can't marry it, or share someone else's. You definitely won't outsmart it, or fake it for more than a few moments. Unfortunately, most people's errant and often infused assumptions about what a quality life is makes achieving one even less likely!

In a Nutshell

Creating and living a quality life requires *three* elements.

First, you must understand how life and living actually works. It's nothing we're taught in school, although it should be. This empowers you to understand its inner workings, and enables you to become creative with them.

Next, you must understand what people who already live truly high-quality lives know that you don't. This allows you to design and create the foundations that a quality life requires to blossom and flourish. If there's one shortcut when it comes to living a high quality life, this is the only one you can expect.

Finally, you must understand what's truly important about you and your life, and interweave your most wondrous passions and desires into its fabric.

Practical Life Design Strategy

You will encounter Practical Life Design Strategy exercises following most chapters in this book. These questions allow you to apply what you've learned to your own life. *Don't skip this step!* You'll use your answers and notes when you design your life plan later. You might want to purchase a *Life Journal* of some sort to record your notes and answers. I personally use a Moleskine® journal mainly for comfort and nostalgic reasons. You can use any style of journal. Keep your journal with you; you never know when something important will pop up in your mind.

On pages 263-267 you will also find user note pages where you can jot quick notes down.

When thinking about what you have just read, and your own life, please explore the following questions.

1.1 Why did you purchase this book?

1.2 Why did you purchase this book now?

1.3 What do you hope to accomplish with this book?

1.4 Are you happy with yourself as an individual?

1.5 Why or why not?

1.6 Are you happy with your life?

1.7 Why or why not?

1.8 Are you the person you envisioned yourself as being earlier in life?

1.9 Why or why not?

1.10 If you were to categorize your overall life on a scale of 1 to 10, with 1 being totally out of control and 10 being perfect contentment, where would you place your life?

1.11 If you were to categorize your quality of life on a scale of 1 to 10, with 1 being poor and 10 being exceptional, where would you place your quality of life?

1.12 What would you say the "cancer" is or was in your life in terms of a life-altering event?

1.13 What about your life do you love?

1.14 What about your life would you do differently?

1.15 What are the most important passions in your life that have nothing to do with other people? (e.g.: painting, children, faith, golfing, sailing, dancing, cooking, etc.)

1.16 When thinking about the driving forces in your life, would you say they tend to be more aligned to satisfying the interests and passions of others or pursuing your own interests and passions?

1.17 What is your definition of a high quality life?

1.18 Name 10 things that you associate with a high quality life.

1.19 Name the most important reasons why you want to transition your life to a higher quality life.

1.20 If you could have a high quality life, what would you be willing to do to keep it?

CHAPTER TWO
IMAGINE

> *"Transformation doesn't simply occur. It first requires a reason and the freedom to react."*
>
> ~ **Ian Breck**

A beautiful life. What an amazing concept! Can you imagine what it would it be like to wake up each morning excited about what the new day would bring? Lunch with special friends, sailing, golfing with family or colleagues, working in the garden, or just reading a book in a hammock are only a few of the ideas that come to mind immediately. Imagine sipping freshly brewed Tarrazu coffee, Bai Hao Yin Zhen tea, or sinfully rich hot cocoa from New York's *Vosges Haut Chocolat* while slipping into a good book from your warm spot under six layers of blankets on a cold, blue, snowy morning. Or, maybe it's a trip to the mountains or the beach with friends that gets you going. Perhaps it's just sitting back and listening to the sounds of nature in your own back yard that turns you on. It might also be about the fantastic career you've worked so hard to discover throughout your life. The idea that you can live a life around your passions and what's important to you is a stretch for many when they consider today's harsh realities. However, more and more, people today are stepping out of their comfort, or *stagnant zones*, as I call them, and doing just that – daring to live their lives in inspired new ways - and loving every step of their new adventures in living!

People are taking back control of their lives, reimagining, and redesigning them more than ever today. It isn't naiveté. It's a realistic, viable, and remarkable option we all have. Life is simply too short to live sub-standard existences. So, why live it foolishly, or by someone else's standards?

Redesigning your life, however, is not without its challenges. For those wanting to take back the control and design of their lives, it can be a journey fraught with peril and frustration. The biggest problem most encounter is the fear they're biting off more than they can chew – and subsequently walking away altogether as they stumble over their fears and lack of knowledge. Is it too complicated? Will your personal baggage thwart your efforts? What will the final result look like? Where do I begin? While these questions are important, they all too often become excuses for doing nothing.

Reimagining and redesigning your life doesn't have to be complicated. It requires a serious commitment, and the understanding that no shortcuts, silver bullets, or quick fixes exist. Redesigning your life isn't a spectator sport - no one can do it for you. It's about being engaged every step of the way and having a willingness to explore your life in sometimes uncomfortable, albeit honest and constructive ways. The reassuring part is that you typically do the tough parts alone, and no one has to know the rare foible or flaw you *may* discover. However, when all is said and done, your improved life quality will reward you many times over.

One of the most common concerns clients express is their fear the baggage they bring with them will somehow detract from, undermine, or inhibit their efforts to create a better life. The baggage you bring to the game is not nearly as important as your willingness to carry it on your back, or at least place it behind, rather than in front of you. Your baggage contains invaluable knowledge, experience, insight, and inspiration that give you and your life depth, and hard-earned motivation along the way.

The most important point to remember is that reimagining your life isn't about undoing, changing, or erasing your past. Your past is a defining part of who you are and cannot be erased. Then again, why would you want to walk away from your life and the lessons it contains? You can, however, make the less attractive elements (and we all have them) of your past less influential and unimportant in a number of ways. Embrace your past and its lessons, and allow it to propel and motivate your journey to a more wonderful life.

Undoubtedly, the most common issue I confront with clients is *unrealistic expectations*. Although a high quality life is better in almost every way than its counterpart, "better" doesn't necessarily mean "no problems or challenges." A healthy life requires problems and challenges to refine and reinforce understandings and strategies. The major advantage of a higher quality life is its far more supportive, nourishing, and protective environment. When problems do arise, the supportive characteristics of a quality life most often provide a softer landing.

Taking Back Control

According to studies, an estimated 93% of all Americans report feeling as if they've lost control of their life at one or more points during their adult years. What does this really mean? It tells us that 7% of Americans are lying. Each of us experiences feelings of losing control at one point or another in our lives. In fact, it's perfectly natural. It's our body's way of telling us the rules and strategies we're using to live our lives aren't keeping up with our environmental realities and demands. For some, it's an occasional encounter, or hiccup. For others, it's more of a chronic condition. The goal is to understand what's really happening - and taking control of your life when it appears to be taking you on one of its psychedelic roller coaster rides.

When it comes to actually losing physical or emotional control of life, humans tend to be a pretty resilient lot. However, feeling as if you're losing control of your life is certainly disconcerting, if not incapacitating to some. As disquieting as it can be, I've found such feelings frequently arise from one of two common scenarios.

The first and most common scenario occurs when we discover our life strategies and rules have been replaced, or hijacked, by someone or something other than ourselves. I refer to this as the *Trojan Horse Syndrome*. It goes something like one day you wake up and realize you're living by someone else's ideals, standards, or expectations. When others impart or inject their rules, strategies, or beliefs into our lives, we tend to respond adversely both psychologically and physiologically as a result of our foreign invader(s). The response we experience is our system telling us it wants the invaders gone because they're uncomfortable, and not a natural part of who we are.

The more common and even more insidious bigger brother of the Trojan Horse Syndrome occurs when we *don't* realize or suspect our lives are being influenced by something or someone else. These influences can originate from someone as close as our partner, or boss, to companies, religions, political organizations, retail stores, and governments that don't even know your name! As it turns out, the world is full of people with a desire to control your thoughts and behaviors for any number of reasons – and it's not as difficult to accomplish as you might think! The key is ensuring you're the one in charge and control of your life and its design.

The next scenario occurs when we discover the strategies and rules we use to live our lives are no longer keeping pace with our reality. In most cases, we have the choice of either 1.) Changing our rules and strategies; or how we live our lives, or 2.) Changing the environment in which we live. In either case, ensuring your life design is up to your reality is an essential part of living well.

Experiencing feelings that you've lost, or are about to lose control of your life can be quite disconcerting, yet also strangely motivating at the same time. According to many High Q people, taking back control of their lives first began with becoming angry at the realization that others are so arrogant to think they have a right to control or define anyone else's life. However, those emotions commonly shift to disheartenment for being able to be controlled by someone or something else in the first place. It happens just this easily - and often without any inkling or realization it's occurring.

So, where does it all begin? Taking back the control of your life begins at the very moment you assume responsibility for the outcomes of your decisions, solutions, design, and problems within your life. It's a powerful commitment that's easy to make, but often difficult to keep.

REIMAGINING YOUR LIFE

It's one thing to *want* to take back control of your life; it's quite another to actually *do* it. Thanks to a remarkable process known as *reimagination*, exploring and refining your life has become much more intuitive, far easier, and dramatically more successful. It's something that should be part of every adult skill set.

Living a life that no longer reflects your passions, dreams and ideals, is a flawed strategy. Reimagining your life in new and exciting ways is how the next chapter of your life begins. Reimagination is a process that enables you to dream and explore what your life would look like if it were designed and lived differently. What would your life look like if you got that pilot's license, your MBA, or perhaps retire to a life of RV'ing through America? How would it work? How would it change? How would it improve? What sacrifices would you have to make? Regardless of the premise, reimagination provides invaluable opportunities to contemplate your life from entirely *different* perspectives. Even more importantly, reimagination is an easy and engaging experience anyone can undertake!

So, who wouldn't jump at the opportunity to take back the control of their life and refine or reinvent it in some way – or at least explore a few options for a lifestyle face-lift of sorts? As it turns out, it's not a natural behavior! Most people require some sort of reason before they begin to question the structure and function of their lives. This usually comes in the form of a life-altering, or at least life-challenging, event. When it comes to toiling with our own lives, we tend not to want to rock the boat when all is moving along nicely – or at least acceptably. Ideally, however, reimagination is something everyone should perform on a regular basis starting at ages 13-14, depending on maturity levels. You are, however, never too old.

When it comes to reimagining your life, I've found there are generally *three* groups of people worth mentioning.

The first group accepts substandard existence as their reality, and does little or nothing to make their lives different or better. They tend to live low quality, depressed existences. These are *martyrs*. The lives of martyrs are built from and around failure and unhappiness. They commonly reinforce their existences with related behaviors and associations. If it's true that misery loves company, you'll undoubtedly find lots of it in the hats of martyrs. Martyrs are important to quality life pursuers because they represent the endgame for individuals who have lost control, meaning, and hope in their lives.

The next group includes those who aren't really sure what about to do with their lives - but are willing to try almost anything with even the remotest possibility of improving them in some way. These individuals spend a great deal of time and money hanging their hopeful hats on spiritualistic teachings, religion, superstition, new age groups, and the latest self-help fads – at least until they fail. While these practices represent powerful frameworks for many people, this particular group looks for quick fixes without serious or prolonged commitment. Their results are almost always less than they expected, which is where problems begin.

I know one woman who wholeheartedly swears the power of garlic – *that is absorbed through her feet in her shoes!* She says it has lowered her blood pressure 20 points and helped her meet her fourth husband! Who am I to argue with success? However, when individuals in this group realize their latest, "big" thing isn't achieving the miraculous and earth-shattering results they expected or were promised, they alter their course immediately and set out to discover the next "big" thing! These are *shoppers*. You've probably known several.

Finally, we arrive at our third group. This group genuinely is interested in living satisfying and rewarding lives, makes the required commitments, and is willing to do what it takes to discover and achieve lives that are more amazing - intelligently. These people aren't simply looking to change their lives, they're looking to become *creative* with them. Those who succeed are known as *High Q people*.

ONE STEP AT A TIME

Making your life better requires you to embrace change as a positive catalyst within your life. Reimagination is about exploring your life in new and exciting ways that are *different*. The process begins by you assuming the responsibility for your life, its design, and outcomes. Once you've made this commitment, you're ready to step into your new role as your life's designer.

Reimagination is a fascinating exercise accomplished through three primary steps.

Step 1: Understanding how life works

Knowing about life and living more completely not only enables you to understand how it all works together, but also empowers you to become creative with the design of your own life. By understanding just a few features of life and living in greater detail, you can make profound changes and contributions to your life and its quality. When it comes to life and living well, you'll discover minuscule adjustments often result in quite profound differences.

In *Section One*, we'll explore life and living.

Step2: Understanding how High Q people think and live

If you want to know more about living an exceptional life, explore the lives of those who live them every day. Despite being as different as you or I, High Q people share specific characteristics that provide the essential foundations high quality lives require to exist and thrive.

In *Section Two*, we'll explore these characteristics in greater detail and discover what they reveal about life and living well.

Step 3: Making it happen!

In *Section Three*, we'll put what you've learned to work within your own life. You'll create a new life plan based on the reimagination of your own life!

Practical Life Design Strategy

When thinking about what you have just read, and your life, please explore the following questions.

2.1 Do you feel that you control your life? If not, explain why.

2.2 Do you feel that forces outside or within yourself limit or inhibit the quality of your life? If so, why?

2.3 How do you believe your knowledge, experiences, and attitudes limit or inhibit your quality of life?

2.4 Do you rely on yourself to achieve happiness or do you base your value and happiness on how others feel about you?

2.5 Does the idea of transitioning your life intimidate or motivate you? Why?

2.6 Does the work associated with transitioning your life intimidate or motivate you? Why?

2.7 Are you most often successful at endeavors you undertake? Why, or why not?

2.8 Are you finding yourself making excuses for not transitioning your life or reasons to transition your life? If so, why?

2.9 What would you do differently if you had life to live over again?

2.10 What do you expect the results of a higher quality life to be within the context of your own life?

Section One - Life Lessons

Life is truly an amazing state of existence. Understanding the language of life, how it develops, and how it's lived are essential first steps toward imagining and designing a life of your own that is even more rewarding.

In the next six chapters, we'll explore the basics of life and living, and reveal the essential elements that define and control the lives we live.

Reader Note…

> *The next six chapters provide essential life and knowledge understandings for anyone wanting to design, live, and maintain a higher quality life. That being said, these chapters provide more in-depth explorations and are somewhat heavier reading than the chapters that follow.*
>
> *If you would prefer to explore these next six chapters after reading the rest of this book, you may jump ahead to Section Two – Life Strategies and return later. Naturally, we suggest a straight-through approach, but the choice is yours.*

Reimagined

CHAPTER THREE
BECOMING YOU

"From the very moment you're born, you begin a journey of becoming you."

~ **Ian Breck**

So, what's this thing we call "life" anyway? After all, if we're going to become creative with something we cannot even see or touch, it would be rather helpful to know a bit more about what it is we're playing with. In reality, few people truly understand what life is all about or how it really "works." When talking about life, we're speaking about its expressive form - not its biological or psychological counterparts. We're most interested in the stuff that provides animation and purpose to our body and self.

Because life just "*is*," we don't really think much about it. In fact, we tend to take it for granted until its existence, functionality, or environment is somehow challenged. Of all we don't understand about life, we do know that living well requires us to understand life well enough to manage and become creative with it. As it turns out, a quality life definitely favors the prepared mind.

Unfortunately, when it comes to understanding life itself, there's not a great deal of information of any real value for the average individual, or even expert for that matter. It's fairly easy, however, to come across philosophical explorations, religious writings, new-age tomes, or just about anything that skirts the fact that we simply don't know a great deal about life as we know or live it.

Describing life, or at least what it's about, is truly an ethereal exercise that reveals the true inefficacy of words. Unlike most things in our world, life has no mass, color, scent, noise, flavor, or texture that defines it. Describing life is akin to describing "balance" – it's virtually impossible to verbalize, yet it's something you recognize instantly when you see it.

Life is what distinguishes you and I from the otherwise barren panorama of interstellar carbon, rock, and iron we call "earth." Life is the most amazing and compelling expression of chemistry. Life is physiology, knowledge, expertise, and free will personified. It's the convergence of all we believe and know. It provides depth, uniqueness, and meaning in a world of sameness. Life is our raison d'être, and gives birth to our intangible yearnings to create, experience, and leverage the stuff of our world. Life's most profound product is *love*. Love enables us to exist within a context far greater than that of ourselves. Love is the only thing that makes us greater than the sum of our parts.

Characterizing life has proven illusive to even the best minds in history. As it turns out, life is most easily understood by what it *creates* - not what it *is*.

Life Cycles

> *"Science and research have given us greater understandings of our world. However, life and living have introduced science to its theoretical limits."*
>
> ~ **Ian Breck**

Squish! Smack! Wah! Welcome home, baby! Now that the formalities and niceties are out of the way, let's suck that mucous from your nose and get on with your new life! Your clock has begun ticking and new ones just like you are popping out every 4.2 seconds. Besides, you only have a little over 3,700 weeks before your tour ends. Let's get started!

Despite the occasional, yet necessary indignity, life is truly a miraculous state of existence. Many scientists believe we start our journey with only three things: hunger pangs, the fear of falling, and the love of our mother. From these foundations, all of who and what we'll become is made possible through learning and experience. We're little more than breathing voids waiting to be filled, shaped, and ultimately experienced by our world. The most successful among us will design their life experience. The least successful will be controlled by theirs. The differences in outcomes are indeed profound.

As an infant, you embark upon an amazing journey that exposes you to more stimulation than you'll encounter at any other point in your life – including death. You're discovering the many people, places, and things of your world while becoming acclimated to something amazingly complex: *language.* You soon discover those twisty pointy things on the end of your arms, and how they bring your world closer. They make people's faces do funny things when they bring eyebrows and nostrils closer for your inspection. You discover they're also great for helping you travel in your big new world. Incidentally, they're excellent for holding that funny fuzzy thing mom and dad call a "*cat.*" You like the cat-thing. How versatile your design is!

You're learning by discovery at this stage in your life. This type of learning enables you learn through experiences, interactions, and experiments. Despite being slower and more demanding than other forms of learning, discovery is by far the most accurate and concise learning method humans employ. As a child, you're endowed with a special lucidity that allows you to discover your world with more accuracy and greater clarity than at any other time in your life. Learning is a quite miraculous process that is directing your development at this age.

Typically from 12 to 16 months of age, infancy yields to toddlerdom. You enter this phase of your life as an explorer in residence. In fact, you're an explorer tour de force among other French words you're likely to hear during your infamous tenure. Your new discovery skills reveal wondrous things about you and your world. Interestingly, you're temporarily more interested in how stuff tastes rather than deriving any real pleasure from what it does at this point. We don't really understand why you do this, and you could care less. All you know is that the cat-thing tastes… *futhy*. At this point, you're all about understanding your world. It's all about discovery. It's all about you.

Only when your discovery skills reach their loftiest levels of proficiency will you be introduced to the word that will forever change your life - "*no!*" This is not a new word to you, nor is it the prettiest one you'll come across. In fact, it's rather harsh. You've heard it many times before. However, now you encounter it along with the unnecessary brutality of getting your hand or butt smacked. Oh, the inhumanity of it all! You hate "no." However, declaring your displeasure too loudly may get your mouth smacked also! You eventually begin equating the word "no" with nothing particularly good, fun, or warm and fuzzy for that matter.

The cat-thing fears you.

The word "no" marks your introduction to the first of many decision-making quandaries within your life. Free will introduces paradox to the word "no." It goes kind of like this: you do something to the big fuzzy cat-thing that makes it let out a rather hideous, but also quite amusing noise! It's entertaining, but again, you really don't know why. It also happens to displease mom greatly for some reason. From out of nowhere, "no!" Apparently, the trick is to determine whether or not the unpleasantries you associate with the word "no" are more compelling than the mind-boggling joy and laughter that pulling those funny triangle thingy's on the top of the cat-thing's head! So, which door do you choose? You really like the sound the cat-thing makes - it makes you laugh. It's now a battle between your free will (*self-determination*) and mom (*self-preserva-*

tion). It's a toughie! It's also a conundrum you'll face untold times throughout the rest of your life. Often times, life becomes a battle between the "right" thing and the "right now" thing. Despite your best efforts, you'll never get it 100% right.

Your impressive discovery skills along with all of the forgiveness your tooth-challenged cuteness avails takes you to about the age of six. You've come a long way, baby. You can now communicate, recognize tens of thousands of objects, walk, demonstrate basic reasoning skills, know what you like, and what you don't. You've become a walking, talking, and thinking machine!

If you think age six is only kid's stuff, think again. Wolfgang Mozart played his first concerts throughout Europe at this age. Shirley Temple won an Oscar for her "lifetime" contribution to film, and Ron Howard started his career as Opie Taylor on the *Andy Griffith Show* at age six. Not to be outdone by modern overachievers, Egypt's Pepi II became the Pharaoh of Egypt at six – and kept his job for another 94 years!

The cat-thing ran away today. Quitter.

You've now started school. Some of it's fun. The kid who sits behind you is a butthead. What? No? Smack! As if it weren't enough to learn a new language in the first place, you're now expected to make decisions about using it too? Really? Seriously? (You'd better explain this to your father when he gets home; he apparently doesn't understand this part.)

You're learning at a feverish pace by age eight – and becoming capable of quite a great deal. Mozart has already completed his first symphony, and comedian Bernie Mac has just given his first stand-up routine at his church. His crowd-pleasing impressions of his grandparents earn him a spanking later that day! By eight years of age, you've learned more than you'll learn in any subsequent eight-year period in your life. You've become proficient at life and living.

At this point, you enjoy reading; but, math - not so much. For the first time in your life, your brain begins feeling full. It's not really "full," it's just really busy. In fact, it's becoming overwhelmed. It requires a more efficient way to deal with the massive amount of knowledge and information you're asking it to process. It needs some form of a "shortcut" to make its job easier, or at least more efficient. Instead of learning by discovery as you've done in the past, you discover a new strategy that you'll use throughout the rest of your life: learning through *decision-making*. It's much faster, but less accurate than learning by discovery. Instead of discovering everything you know, you begin making educated guesses based on your knowledge, experience, and assumptions. Although it's quicker, this new learning strategy will also cause you a great deal of problems in the future. In many cases, your decision-making skills will become the rope you'll hang yourself with.

Unlike most things that benefit from experience, decision-making becomes less accurate as we grow older. "Close enough" often becomes "good enough." Unfortunately, decision-making eventually becomes an exercise of proximity rather than one of accuracy. I sincerely hope you'll outgrow this misguided, reckless, and dangerous strategy someday. (You won't.)

As you grow, your discovery skills begin to atrophy thanks to your increasing reliance on decision-making as your primary learning strategy. Decision-making turns out to be far more efficient than discovery despite its somewhat compromised accuracy. However, you don't really care about that right now - you're only eight years old. The cat-thing has been replaced by a sister-thing. She hates you too.

You're now noticing the other sex. Not that you really know what "sex" is beyond gender, you just know she's a girl, he's a boy, and somehow the two are different. For now, that's really all that matters. All you know is that girls are yucky and boys stink. However, in the back of your mind, you also realize that you kind of like yucky and/or stinky people – another conundrum that will follow you throughout life.

Combine your newfound curiosity with your hectic life, less accurate learning, immature problem solving skills and solution creation abilities, and you have the makings of a perfect storm. However, you don't quite realize this yet, despite constant reminders from mom and dad that you're not quite as smart as you think you are. Whatever. They're old – almost 30! You're growing. You begin interacting with others in new ways. You're experiencing and developing experience. Everything you've learned and experienced to this point is forming the foundation of your "*self.*"

So, there you have it! We've just run through the script of your life, and how it's formed. From the very moment you enter this world, you begin the development of a rather remarkable existence forged quite humbly from only three instincts. From that point forward, your life is shaped by the knowledge you gain, the experiences you encounter, the decisions you make, and the problems you solve. Your "self" is forming and evolving more quickly now. You're becoming you.

You should now be able to form a practical working definition of "life" based on what you've just explored. The answer can be found in what you've just read. Before turning to the next page, try to define life based on what you've learned to this point.

TURN THE PAGE FOR MY DEFINITION OF LIFE.

LIFE…

…the physical manifestation of your knowledge, experience, expertise, decisions, solutions, passions, and free will. Your life is the perfect reflection of everything you!

ON THE EDGE…

Let's jump into the world of research for a quick aside about human development.

Children follow a relatively constant learning curve driven by their innate curiosity along with an uncompromising sense of discovery, wonder, awe, and amazement. Powerful learning and thinking skills enable children to process their world and extract knowledge from their experiences with remarkable efficiency and precision. These skills include powerful processes such as decision-making, problem-solving, solution creation, and many other activities. However, infants appear to have an almost instinctual familiarity and primitive command of complex life concepts including relationships, trust, and even love and insecurity at only a few weeks of age. Is there something happening during infancy we don't understand? I believe the answer might be *yes*.

Many scientists believe we learn all we know from the experiences we encounter from the moment we're born. According to conventional thought, we're born only with the instincts of hunger pangs, fear of falling, and the love of our mother. Frankly, too many behaviors infants exhibit cast doubts on such thinking. Questions like why twins and siblings from the same parents often have dissimilar personalities, why an infant is repelled or attracted to someone they've never met, or why infants in the womb respond when they experience music have always piqued my curiosity.

I developed *x-Seed theory*, which suggests we're born with a rather extensive, albeit primitive, set of pre-defined instinctual life skills that are actionable and available to us before birth. As we grow and develop, our "x-seeds" become more refined, eventually becoming the formalized foundations of our cognitive and behavioral skill sets and strategies.

If x-seed theory proves true, it would force us to rethink how we learn, grow, and what really influences cognitive performance. This would also change education and even how we treat psychological and cognitive dysfunction. It provides a compelling point for exploration, discussion, and hopefully, future research.

What It Means

Life is an absolutely mind-boggling state of existence. The idea that carbon life forms such as us could become intelligently actionable is beyond imagination. The only things close to being as brilliant as life itself are the processes that enable us to live the lives we do.

As young children, we begin exploring our new world and learning with a precision that will never be greater. As we grow, we adopt new strategies to interact with our world more efficiently. Some are brilliant. Others are compromises. However, once we develop greater decision-making skills at about age seven, we cease being spoon-fed carbon life forms and begin our role as master, gatekeeper, and the ultimate designer of our own lives. This is where the true brilliance of life and living comes into its own – and when parenthood draws closer to the end of its most influential period.

The most amazing elements of the happiest lives are the same ones that make the world amazing to children. These include curiosity, awe, discovery, creativity, and exploration. The same things that drive and inspire us as children, inspire the happiest and healthiest adult lives. However, as life becomes more complex and busy, these characteristics become less prominent and fade – and we often fail to thrive because of it.

The first secret of a wonderful life is never to become too old to experience a happy childhood!

Practical Life Design Strategy

When thinking about what you have just read, and your life, please explore the following questions.

3.1 Why do our years as a child matter so much?

3.2 What do you think the impact to a child would be if their parents had a loving relationship? A violent relationship? He or she had no love expressed toward them?

3.3 How does it affect a child when they are exposed to something?

3.4 How does it affect a child when they are not exposed to something?

3.5 Do you think it's possible to "engineer" a child's existence in a way that influences their entire life? Why?

3.6 When thinking about question 3.5, what would the benefits and detriments be of "engineering" a child's life?

3.7 When we say "life," what are we are really talking about?

3.8 Name five (5) ways our childhood years influence how we see and perceive our world?

3.9 How can our childhood years influence how we see and perceive others?

3.10 Thinking about you as a person, do you believe you have been more influenced, either good or bad, by your innate intelligence (nature) or your personal experiences (nurture) – and why?

3.11 When thinking about your answers to question 3.10, how would that change the way you would raise a child?

3.12 When thinking about your answers to question 3.10, how would that change how you would treat your life partner?

3.13 When thinking about your answers to question 3.10, how would that change the way you would see another employee or colleague?

3.14 When thinking about your answers to question 3.10, how would that change the way you treat an elderly person?

3.15 Thinking of people you know who live high quality lives, what about them stands out to you?

3.16 Thinking of people you know who live high quality lives, what things about them do you admire and criticize?

3.17 Thinking about yourself in comparison to others who you believe live high quality lives, what are the differences you see?

3.18 On a scale from 1 (poor) to 10 (exceptional), how would you rate your problem-solving ability? Why?

3.19 On a scale from 1 (poor) to 10 (exceptional), how would you rate your solution creation ability? Why?

3.20 On a scale from 1 (poor) to 10 (exceptional), how would you rate your decision-making ability? Why?

3.21 How do your decisions affect your life?

3.22 How do your decisions affect the lives of others?

3.23 When we talk about learning using discovery, what are we talking about?

3.24 When we talk about learning using decision-making, what are we talking about?

3.25 Many scientists believe that decision-making becomes less accurate as we mature. Why?

3.26 As we mature, we rely less and less on discovery as a learning model. What are the impacts of this and what can be done to mitigate them?

CHAPTER FOUR
A RIDICULOUSLY SHORT COURSE IN KNOWLEDGE

> *"For many today, reasoning has become an exercise of justifying what they already believe or want others to think instead of ensuring what they believe is accurate, truthful, and just."*
>
> ~ **Ian Breck**

Knowledge is the most important and powerful asset we possess. Without it, nothing – including life itself – is possible. Nothing else in the world even remotely compares to knowledge in terms of value, power, and potential. People undertake unimaginable travails to acquire and master it. Organizations do almost anything to possess and transform it into profitable and actionable assets, despite being yoked with the reality they can do absolutely nothing to retain or preserve it. These are the realities of this ultra-powerful, dynamic, yet intangible force of life.

As remarkably powerful as knowledge is, the sad irony is that very few people have any realistic idea of what it's about. Adding salt to the wound is the fact that knowledge suffers from having no standardized definition. Most definitions of knowledge are either incorrect or misleading. Because of problems like these, very few people understand the true nature, dynamics, and mechanics of knowledge and expertise. That's right – we're woefully ignorant and uninformed about the core foundation of our very existence.

You would think something with the strategic value and consequence of knowledge and expertise would be cloaked in relentless research. In reality, the true leading edge research isn't happening within or being sponsored by large companies or governments. It's conducted almost exclusively by small, typically independent, researchers.

Of all we don't understand about knowledge and expertise, we know knowledge, learning, and life quality are inextricably linked. The quality of your decisions and solutions contribute diametrically to your life experience.

OF KNOWLEDGE

So, what is knowledge - really? Is it information, data, or perhaps something else? In a nutshell, knowledge is the conceptual understanding that remains *after* you process, refine, and organize information, data, and other stimuli. In other words, it's not the flour, water, chocolate, eggs, oil, cocoa, or baking powder. It's the cake that results from them. It's that simple – albeit complex at the same time.

If you pick up a particular animal and it bites you, you'll associate that animal (and probably others like it) as being potentially dangerous. Your perceptions, experiences, and beliefs of that particular animal and those like it form your conceptual understanding of it. Your conceptual understanding of anything becomes your knowledge of it.

Throughout life, we acquire, leverage, and create staggering amounts of information, data, knowledge and expertise. Most people consider the human body a "living" machine. In reality, we're "knowledge leveraging" machines. Without the ability to process massive amounts of knowledge and expertise, we simply couldn't exist. On an average day, you'll make between 40,000 and 100,000 decisions using the knowledge you possess, acquire, and create. You're constantly encountering new experiences and environments that demand translation, consideration, and interaction. We're all truly amazing knowledge-leveraging beings thanks to our brain's remarkable capacity to leverage what we know and experience.

Our brains are beyond extraordinary in terms of functionality, complexity, and physiology. Think of your brain as a massive computer with one exception – it's light years more advanced in every possible way. Your brain processes more information faster, possesses superior reasoning and logic facilities, initiates, controls, and ends activities; and produces chemicals essential for management and maintenance of your body. Your brain also manages your senses and provides remarkably sophisticated functionalities like recognition, language, and speech. It manages emotions, instinctual and non-instinctual behaviors, controls autonomic systems that regulate your internal organs and systems, and makes consciousness and conscience possible. Even the most sophisticated computers in the world, including IBM's Deep Blue®, can't remotely begin to compete with the massively parallel potential of your amazing three-pound brain.

Aside from the unimaginable physiology of the brain, many believe its most impressive product is the *mind*. Many disagree even today as to what the "mind" really is in precise terms. This, however, isn't anything new. In the 17th century, Rene Descartes and the Catholic Church had a legendary spat over this very issue when Descartes introduced his heretical concept of *dualism* – the innate separation of the brain (body) and the mind (soul). The Catholic Church was not amused. It conceded the body to science, but the mind and soul were to remain the exclusive domain of the Church!

So, what's your "*mind?*" Your mind is the conscious manifestation of intelligent thought and reasoning by your brain.

Your mind is remarkable on so many levels. First, it creates and manages what you do, how you think, who you are, what you believe, your passions, your loves, and everything intangible about you and how you perceive your world. Now, if you think we're going to enter a dissertation about the human brain and its systems, don't worry! Despite tremendous advances in our understandings, the human brain holds its most profound secrets quite closely. We still haven't come remotely close to understanding the precise inner workings of this mysterious organ. Anyone who tells you differently is pulling your medulla oblongata.

When I first began my career as a professional knowledge engineer, understanding the brain and its inner workings represented the Holy Grail for many of us. I absorbed absolutely everything I could about the brain – both the true and speculative stuff alike. In the end, the most we walked away with were conjecture headaches and the occasional hangover. Despite our advancing knowledge, we still understand comparatively little about the mystery wrapped within our cranium.

Thankfully, the brain really wasn't that important to my work. I was mostly interested in its byproducts – knowledge and expertise. As I began exploring the two more intently, I found myself curious, surprised, and somehow inspired by how closely associated knowledge and expertise were to human life and its quality. You see, we place a great deal of emphasis on first-degree knowledge like education, training, and experience – and these do play truly significant roles in our lives. However, it's second-degree knowledge, or the benefits we derive from *using* knowledge, that provides the greatest benefits we receive from knowledge and expertise. In other words, life quality is more about how effectively we *use* the knowledge we possess, rather than what we "know." In the end, the quality of our decisions, solutions, and problem-solving capabilities are far more important to our quality of life than that Master's degree hanging on the wall.

To make this more understandable, we need look no further than a typical saltshaker. Salt is a ubiquitous seasoning – it's everywhere and used in almost everything. However, what it contributes to your quality of life determines whether it is good or bad for you. If you have normal blood pressure, some salt is fine and quite tasty. However, if you have high blood pressure, salt becomes a dangerous antagonist. Salt never changes. How we react to it does. In this case, the result (benefit or detriment) we receive from anything (e.g. our ability to leverage knowledge) determines how it affects the quality of our lives.

I discovered early on the role and staggering influence that second-degree knowledge contributes to overall life quality. Bad decisions, poor solutions, and inadequate problem solving are major inhibitors of life quality. How much of an inhibitor? In my professional estimation, second-degree knowledge is responsible for upwards of 81-94% of life quality. Because of this, learning about knowledge isn't simply about understanding the mechanics of knowledge; it's about understanding how to use the knowledge you possess better and smarter.

KNOWLEDGE 101

Each and every day in the life of your brain and mind is consumed with the responsibilities of discovering, acquiring, creating, and leveraging the knowledge required to keep life running smoothly and predictably. From your mind's point of view, this is the meaning of life.

As you might expect, the interactive dance between you and your world is far more complex than mere synaptic connections, enzymes, and free will. Life represents not only an animated state of existence, but also an interactive one that's made possible by your ability to leverage knowledge, expertise, stimuli, and your ability to use them to interact with your environment. In order to survive and thrive, decisions are made, solutions are created, and problems are solved using your knowledge, experience, and other cognitive skills. When all is working well together, we get along quite nicely with little drama. However, when even one element is compromised, the entire experience of life and living can fall apart suddenly and without warning.

So, what keeps everything playing well together? Your incredibly sexy and sensuous brain! The life you live and experience is found at the junction of your brain, your mind, and your world. Quite frankly, understanding the brain and all of the cool things it's about is well beyond my expertise and the scope of this book. However, if you're interested in learning more about your brain, I recommend *The Owner's Manual for the Brain* by Pierce J. Howard. Ph.D. (ISBN: 1-885167-38-5). It's a great reference for anyone wanting to know more about their most intriguing organ.

Now that you understand a bit more about knowledge and how important it is to life and living well, it's time to learn a bit more about how it all really works together.

Have you ever wondered how you really use your knowledge? Most people are surprised to learn that much of our cognitive functionality is focused around two features of our minds – our *knowledge base* and *inference mechanism*.

(Don't be afraid – these are two truly fascinating features you'll really want to understand!)

The Knowledge Base

When you learn, experience, or do absolutely anything, your brain stores the resulting knowledge in something called your *knowledge base*. Think of it like the hard drive in your computer – only much cooler! Understanding the inner mechanics of your knowledge base reveals powerful clues about how we use knowledge.

Your knowledge base is a knowledge warehouse of sorts that stores the knowledge you use and create every day. While knowledge is categorized in several ways, most scientists today group knowledge into one of four major categories.

Declarative knowledge is not so much knowledge as statements - but not necessarily ones of fact. You can look to the sky and tell your friends it's blue. You can also tell them it's green, purple, or chartreuse! That's the problem with declarative knowledge - it doesn't require or suggest any particular critical processing, thought, rationalization, or truth. It's simply statements. Its truthfulness is always suspect and should always be considered potentially false or potentially flawed without further validation. On the other hand, declarative knowledge is highly efficient in terms of processing and recall. It's why recognition and response are such extremely fast processes.

Procedural knowledge is a more complex knowledge type. Procedural knowledge is akin to knowing *how* to do something. For example, I can show you how to change a car tire. This doesn't mean that I'm a tire-changing expert - I'm not. It simply means that I know the basic tasks required to change a tire. Procedural knowledge doesn't require a great deal of in-depth knowledge or understanding. It only communicates or implies *how* a specific task is performed.

Semantic knowledge is the mother lode of all knowledge. If you have semantic knowledge about something, you not only know how to do it, but also understand the why's, terminology, foundational concepts, and background knowledge that supports what you know. The differentiating characteristic about semantic knowledge is it requires you to have some degree of *experience* with a particular domain of expertise. Semantic knowledge, when combined with experience, transforms *knowledge* into *expertise*, and *novices* into *experts*.

Episodic knowledge is not really of great concern or usefulness on a daily basis. I've added it only to complete the set of knowledge types. If you've ever heard your grandparents say something like, "*Well, I remember when...,*" you've experienced episodic knowledge first hand. Generally, episodic knowledge resides in long-term memory and is so incomplete or highly compiled that it's of little use for anything we're really interested in doing. Even as a knowledge engineer, I consider episodic knowledge largely "junk" knowledge that's seen its better days as far as usefulness; although it does have limited, albeit esoteric uses in specialized forensic knowledge applications.

By recognizing various knowledge types, you can evaluate each type's strengths and weaknesses when you encounter them. If you want to learn about something, ideally you want to tap into the mind of someone with semantic knowledge (an *expert*) as opposed to someone with lesser knowledge types. However, in a pinch, someone with procedural knowledge just might do.

As we continue learning and gaining experience by using our knowledge and expertise, far deeper understandings emerge. By combining knowledge and experience, we develop expertise. Expertise is knowledge that is more complete and refined thanks to experience. Those who possess significant expertise in a particular area of knowledge (*domain*) are considered experts.

So, how does all of your knowledge get loaded into your knowledge base? You acquire the knowledge you possess one experience at a time starting at the very moment you're born. Can you understand how knowledge, life, and living are inextricably linked? One cannot exist without the other, although both exist for the benefit of each other.

We acquire knowledge and expertise through learning, listening, watching, doing, teaching, and otherwise experiencing our world. As you trek through life, everything about you becomes a part of your knowledge base. It's truly overwhelming how much we really do accomplish and the amount of knowledge we leverage on a daily basis, let alone a lifetime.

Here's something even more important to remember about your mind, brain, and life: *Junk in - Junk out*. It's really that simple. When you introduce knowledge into your life that's flawed, inaccurate, or incomplete, your brain and mind uses that knowledge to make the decisions, create solutions, and solve problems that ultimately define your life. Your brain works with what you provide it. It doesn't know the difference between perfect and junk knowledge. Poor knowledge is something you strive to eliminate before it becomes a part of your knowledge base and life.

Despite storing masses of knowledge and expertise, your knowledge base is, well... *dumb!* Although your knowledge base stores massive amounts of knowledge and expertise, it possesses no capacity to do anything with it. That's right - all of your hard-earned knowledge and expertise are just sitting there in a puddle otherwise useless. I tell my clients to think of their knowledge base as a file cabinet – lots of stuff in there just waiting to be used – if it can be found! The problem is that when we acquire knowledge, it gets tossed into the pot with everything else in an almost willy-nilly fashion. It's a real mess inside our knowledge base. If organization were left to our knowledge base, we would indeed be in serious trouble.

So, how do we keep our knowledge straight? For many years, scientists considered "*memory*" as the actual filing cabinet of our knowledge. Today, the knowledge base is seen as a separate entity from memory entirely. While our knowledge base stores knowledge and expertise, our memory provides the functionality to organize, locate, and gather the knowledge we require for functions like decision-making, problem-solving, solution creation, and other cognitive activities like recognition and communication. More simply put, our memory is what makes it possible for us to *remember*.

Your memory is your brain's knowledge manager. It keeps the knowledge you use available and ready for action. It knows when and where to look for most of the knowledge you possess – even the stuff you rarely use. If it cannot find what it needs, it signals you to acquire new knowledge. Sometimes it makes a best effort to develop a plausible solution based on what it already knows – and sometimes it simply doesn't care!

Memory comes in two primary flavors, *short-term* and *long-term*.

Short-term memory is used for instantaneous processes like recognition. It gathers and manages knowledge used from mere milliseconds to rarely longer than two minutes. Once used, it tosses it aside and prepares for the next task. Scientists have begun to classify one subtype of short-term memory as "*working*" memory. Working memory is a super-short lived "scratch pad" of sorts used to store numbers (rarely more than 7 items), and other frequently used bits of information. A major problem with short-term memory is that its performance tends to decline with age. This is why older people, or those who experience stress, anxiety, or disease tend to forget things more easily.

Long-term memory is far more complex. Scientists divide long-term memory into one of two primary subgroups: *explicit* and *implicit*. Explicit memory requires conscious thought in order to be recalled. We access explicit memory when we "remember" anything. Implicit memory, on the other hand, is a far more automatic and instinctual type of memory that enables us to act and react with little or no thought. Language, reflexes, along with other highly compiled and automatic behaviors like many of the processes required to perform activities like driving a car or riding a bicycle are common examples of implicit memory application.

Now that you understand a few basics about how you store and manage knowledge and expertise, it's time to see how we use them in real life. This is where your second knowledge system comes into play: *inference*.

The Inference Mechanism

Your inference mechanism provides your capability to think and interact. Your inference mechanism applies rules and heuristics (*strategies*) to the knowledge and expertise from within your knowledge base and external stimuli. Inference allows you to leverage knowledge, information, and stimuli in ways that enable you to think, explore, discover, apply, and create new knowledge required to make decisions, create solutions, solve problems, and much more. In short, inference makes you *actionable*.

Your inference mechanism transforms knowledge to life. To see inference in action, let's explore what happens when you consider an electrical outlet. Your mind processes the scene something like this:

That is an electrical outlet. IF I stick my fingers in it, THEN I will probably be shocked and possibly harmed or killed. THEREFORE, I will not stick my finger in it!

The IF's, THEN's and THEREFORE's of your life (*reasoning*) are made possible by your inference mechanism. In this example, free will prompts your inference mechanism to command your memory to retrieve all necessary knowledge from your knowledge base required to recognize an electrical outlet. It then determines what might happen IF you touch the outlet by rationalizing that knowledge. Your inference mechanism runs through many potential possibilities based on your memory recall and determines the worst-case scenario. It THEN concludes that sticking your finger in the outlet might cause you harm - and THEREFORE decides to stop you from sticking your finger in the outlet. Significant amounts of processing occur in mere milliseconds thanks to the various systems of your mind working together. However, it has to be fast. You rely on your inference mechanism to make as many as 100,000 decisions each day! That's more than one decision every second!

When you consider or ponder anything, your inference mechanism works with your memory and knowledge base to make sense of your world and enable you to *interact* with it. Your knowledge base, inference mechanism, and memory are tools that make interactive life possible. These are powerful components of the truly remarkable and brilliant design of you.

However, if these things are so powerful and miraculous, why do we make mistakes?

When the Bough Breaks

We've all been there. A decision blows up in your face at the worst possible moment. Your child makes some horrendous blunder and you stand there wondering what just happened. You solve a problem perfectly - except it wasn't the exact one you were asked to solve. There are so many times when we make mistakes and sit there dumbfounded wondering what just happened. It would be great to have a way to understand what went wrong – or possibly how to correct or avoid it in the first place. Because you know a bit more about knowledge and how it's managed, you also have a map to many of the mysteries behind life's unintended consequences.

When we do something incorrectly, or expect something to be one way, but it turns out to be another, the "mistake" is often attributable to one of two problems: *compromised knowledge* or *compromised inference*. In other words, most things go awry when either we have inaccurate or incomplete knowledge, or we process the knowledge we have incorrectly for some reason. The key to understanding what's happening is being able to identify the problem and its cause.

When life throws you curve balls, like a decision or solution you created that just didn't work out as expected, compromised knowledge is often the culprit. Compromised knowledge is knowledge that is incorrect, incomplete, biased, or simply inaccurate for one reason or another. When compromised knowledge makes its way into your solutions, decisions, and problems, the results vary from mildly annoying to potentially cataclysmic. The best way to ensure compromised knowledge doesn't contaminate your life is to ensure the knowledge you use is accurate and complete from the start. In other words, acquire the most concise, accurate, and complete knowledge possible. If the knowledge is suspect ("at risk"), ask questions until you are satisfied that what you're working with is accurate, complete, and otherwise usable.

Compromised inference is the next most common, but far more insidious offender. Stress and anxiety are arguably the two most common and potentially destructive inference inhibitors of thinking clearly. When we talk about stress and anxiety, we're not talking about normal stresses we experience in everyday life. We're talking about forms of stress and anxiety that are so excessive they cause you to respond beyond your cognitive capacity and overflow into an adverse physiological response. Bills, politics, pressures, kids, relationships, parents, career, financial difficulties and more can push you over the top in terms of your capacity to leverage knowledge and interact with your world effectively. When this happens, your inference mechanism can become highly erratic and strained – and your world can turn upside down because of it.

One particularly troubling example of impaired inference performance is becoming more commonplace as social pressures and fears increase. Although this can occur in any environment including the home, we'll explore the workplace, where it's becoming increasingly prevalent.

When someone pressures you using Machiavellian or otherwise high-pressure management or manipulation, your inference capacity is impacted *profoundly*. No one is exempt from the influences of such behaviors. "*Loading*," as it's known, might only occur occasionally, or may be a permanent feature of any environment. Unfortunately, these highly destructive behaviors result in a stressful, hostile, and toxic environments that are exceedingly damaging to human inference capacity and cognitive performance. We categorize these primitive strategies as *caustic-point behaviors*, or "*CPB's*."

In addition to being extraordinarily damaging on every conceivable level, caustic-point behaviors are considered abusive by most leading organizations today. While such behaviors reveal the perpetrator's truly incompetent character, they're also highly destructive to those on the receiving end. In practical terms, caustic-point behaviors reduce the inferential capacity of the average individual by up to 93%. Even more alarming is that the recovery length from any single CPB event averages about *46 times the duration of the event itself.* If you're in a meeting for only fifteen minutes (or one minute - caustic-point damage is calculated in sixty minute intervals), you'll not return to full inferential integrity and capacity for about 46 *hours!* Multiple encounters? Sixty-one minutes? New events don't simply start the clock over again - they *multiply* each event's recovery length by about a factor that ranges from 2.5-14.6 times depending on the duration and frequency of each occurrence. That's quite a long, and entirely unacceptable time to lose significant cognitive performance for an individual or an organization. It's even more unacceptable when you realize it's induced by someone else's ignorance and incompetence.

In addition to issues like stress and anxiety, compromised inference also has other sources. Physiological dysfunction, confusion, distractions, chemistry, environments, excitement, or simply not knowing the "rules of the game" can severely compromise your inference capacity. The fact that it's Friday, you have a date tonight, you're upset with the boss, the boss is upset with you, the football game is on, the kids are screaming, or the fact that you hate Monday's are often more than enough to tilt the scales of clarity and subvert the integrity of our inference capability. When I have a looming golf game, I'm admittedly not at my best as I look forward to not being my best on the golf course later that day! As it turns out, humans are a terribly fickle bunch – and it shows in the quality of our decisions, the solutions we create, and the problems we solve when we're not in our best form.

If you believe inference is inhibited exclusively by organic influences such as stress and anxiety, think again. Interfering with your inference is big business today. Expert guns are ready and more than willing to manipulate and influence your inference – and they're exceptionally good at it. The "art" of selling and advertising is based almost entirely on manipulating how and what you think. So is politics, magic, business, and even religion. If you can be persuaded to think a specific way about anything, your persuaders are more likely to influence your personal behaviors including purchasing, voting, believing, giving, or acting in one way or another. Don't think that those videos of abused puppies by rescue organizations at dinnertime aren't designed to guilt or appall you into giving. They're very aware of how you're wired.

In industries like advertising, business, and politics, manipulating the truth in imaginative ways that entice you into thinking and behaving in predictable ways is a highly valued capability today. Is it deception? In many cases, the answer is yes. However, in other ways it's simply a way of educating and informing consumers. Whether or not the intent of anything is deceptive can be identified by determining what it is you're being "sold," and if the sellers are expanding your intelligence with accurate and complete knowledge, or are manipulating your ignorance of a particular topic. I call this the "*deception/education test.*"

A great example of deception versus education can be seen in political campaign ads. Watch a few days worth of political ads, and explore each ad more closely on sites like FactCheck.org. Over a five-day period, *100% of all political ads I viewed in Indiana were either overtly misleading or blatantly untruthful.* In America, we have truth in advertising and lending, but not in campaigning. If you were in a business, such behavior is called fraud and theft by deception. If you're in politics, it's just another day at the office.

Compromised knowledge and inference can also be influenced by physiological and psychological issues including illness, depression, and physiological conditions affecting our chemistry in ways that wreak havoc on our minds and bodies. Unfortunately, many of these conditions are being misdiagnosed or over diagnosed. According to a CNN report (*"Half of Alzheimer's cases misdiagnosed"* February 2011), an astonishing number of Alzheimer's patients are being misdiagnosed with this life-altering disease. In the end, the definitive diagnostic method for Alzheimer's remains the autopsy. As it turns out, other issues that mimic the symptoms of Alzheimer's are often ignored.

One of the most common oversights in terms of cognitive inhibitors is a simple, but often overlooked condition – Vitamin B12 deficiency (*hypocobalaminemia*). For many, especially more mature adults, they are no longer able to absorb enough vitamin B12 from their diet. The results of B12 deficiency include dramatically reduced cognitive capacity and aging of the brain. It can also result in anemia, muscle weakness, fatigue, shakiness, unsteady gait, incontinence, low blood pressure, depression, and other mood disorders, in addition to cognitive problems including memory dysfunction. Millions of seniors are misdiagnosed by physicians every year with life-altering diseases like Alzheimer's because a simple blood test was never performed. Testing for Vitamin B12 should be a first line test for anyone experiencing cognitive dysfunction at *any* age. Ask for it from your physician.

Trouble in River City

When you suspect your cognitive capacity may be compromised in some way – stop! Consider the decision you're making or the problem you're trying to solve, and determine what might be influencing your thinking adversely - including your confidence in the knowledge you're using to make your decision. Things like impatience, personal bias, and pressures wreak havoc on decision-making accuracy. Stop, evaluate, and eliminate detrimental influences affecting your decisions before moving ahead. When I can't resolve my concerns, I wait to make my decision or solve my problem until a point where my confidence is satisfied. "I don't know yet," is a perfectly acceptable answer. If that won't do, "no" is always the best answer. Until you have the confidence in the knowledge and inference you need to make an informed decision, "no" is always the right answer.

The first step of any decision, solution, or problem to be solved is to ensure the knowledge you're using is accurate and complete. The next step is determining whether your thought processes are accurate, rational, and devoid of undue or inappropriate influence. Knowledge integrity and inference quality are referred to collectively as "*basis.*" Whether a single incident, or life-changing event, when the basis of any decision, solution or problem is compromised, so too is the result. There are no exceptions to this rule.

Those under extreme stress are most prone to errors and misjudgments. This problem is made worse by individuals who develop coping mechanisms that make it virtually impossible to recognize when they're not in the game. Because of this, I always want to know the basis of every decision or solution of any significance. If I'm the one making a decision, I double-check the basis of my decision or solution. If someone else is making the decision, creating a solution, or solving a problem that affects me in any way, I want to know the quality of his or her thinking also. Without knowing these things, I simply pick up my ball and go home.

I have no problems questioning the basis of any decision, where the knowledge came from, and the inference fundamentals. It's become second nature to me - almost like wearing a seatbelt. It's not a vulgar interrogatory. I've mastered how to question others in a positive, informative, and polite way that doesn't make them feel as if I'm questioning their integrity or intelligence – I'm not. I've found that people who present well-thought out decisions are often eager to explain the knowledge and reasoning behind those decisions – and I value this as a learning opportunity for myself and others. On the other hand, those who are evasive, secretive, or vague about the basis of their decisions and solutions should always be considered unsafe. Experience has shown me they often times are. In the end, the degree of confidence I place with any decision or solution determines the confidence and weight I give to outcomes and those who provide them.

THE LEADING EDGE

The interactions between your knowledge base and inference mechanism are not merely hypothetical events – you can actually feel them! Your brain devotes so much energy to this interaction that you can feel it when it occurs. When answering the following questions, pay close attention to how your head physically feels as your brain responds:

- What is the square root of 26?
- In the Periodic Table of Elements, what element is "AU?"
- Who was the president five presidents ago?

Did you feel your body respond? It's a short intense burst. You're feeling your brain marshaling all of the energy and resources to answer these questions. Your brain can't help itself – it's the only human organ born with a natural addiction: *problem solving*.

The importance of using knowledge well is not just about accurate decisions, appropriate solutions, and effective problem solving. It's also about how these activities influence the quality of your life. Bad decisions set you back in life and diminish your potential. Good decisions move you ahead and give you wings. Solving problems poorly creates more problems. Solving problems well creates new understandings, tools, and the confidence you need to further define yourself and enhance the quality of your life. Poor solutions not only speak for themselves, but also say a great deal about you. Great solutions make life easier and demonstrate your value. In the end, your ability to use knowledge more effectively not only makes life easier and increases your sense of well-being, but is also the single most important contributor to your quality of your life you control.

So, why is all of this so important? Your knowledge, decisions, solutions, and how you interact with your world come together to form something even more amazing… your "*self*."

WHERE IT FITS

Knowledge, expertise, and experience are inextricably linked to your development and quality of life. Understanding more about them, and the ways they fail provides invaluable insights into life and living.

From a quality life perspective, leveraging the nature of knowledge allows you to leverage it more effectively and intelligently – and ultimately become creative with it. It also helps you know where to discover answers when life throws you curveballs!

Practical Life Design Strategy

When thinking about what you have just read, and your life, please explore the following questions.

4.1 What is knowledge?

4.2 How is knowledge acquired?

4.3 Describe the four types of knowledge, along with why they are categorized how they are in your life.

4.4 Describe at least three examples of each type of knowledge that you use. (E.g. declarative – to recognize the current weather, etc.)

4.5 Describe at least three different examples from question 4.3 of each type of knowledge that others use. (E.g. declarative – to tell me what their schedule is, etc.)

4.6 What are the strengths and weaknesses of procedural knowledge?

4.7 Which knowledge type is the best – and why?

4.8 What makes a doctor a doctor?

4.9 What are the three mechanisms we use to think and reason?

4.10 Describe each of these mechanisms, what they do, and why they are important.

4.11 If you have problems remembering things, what are the possible causes?

4.12 What are the differences between your knowledge base and your memory?

4.13 When a child makes a mistake, what can possibly be the reason(s)?

4.14 When an adult makes a mistake, what can possibly be the reason(s)?

4.15 How is knowledge and information added to your knowledge base?

4.16 How do political advertisements work?

4.17 What is the role of your inference mechanism?

4.18 You've just made a "bad" decision. How might it have happened?

4.19 You have a daughter, who is 12 years old, tells you she is in love with the neighbor boy and wants to marry him. Can you describe her thought process, and what you would do to refine it?

4.20 You have a gathering of friends. To ensure that everyone has fun, you have some games in mind. When it comes time to play, no one seems that interested in playing and stands around talking instead. You are disappointed. Describe what happened in terms of your knowledge base, inference, and memory.

4.21 You have a friend who is making decisions about her life because she is experiencing relationship problems. Describe what may be happening with her in terms of her knowledge base, inference and memory – and possible actions you can take to ease her burden.

4.22 You are working with a colleague whose work is not as good as you have known it to be in the past. It is affecting the success of your project. Describe what may be happening with him or her in terms of knowledge base, inference and memory – and ways to mitigate the poor performance of your colleague and to ensure the success of the project.

4.23 You tell your infant child not to do something and they do it anyway. Describe what may be happening in terms of his or her knowledge base, inference and memory – and what you can do to refine it.

4.24 You are afraid of heights – you have acrophobia. You understand that your acrophobia is an irrational or excessive fear. However, that doesn't matter. Describe what may be happening in terms of your knowledge base, inference and memory – and what you might do to refine it.

4.25 Your boss just called you on the carpet for some work you did that didn't meet his expectations. Describe what may have happened in terms of your knowledge base, inference and memory – and what you can do to refine it.

4.26 You absolutely love the Lexus your neighbor drives. You go to the dealership and the salesperson tells you that if you buy today, he will give you an additional $1,000 off. What is he really doing? What is your response - and why?

4.27 Your child is helping you water and fertilize the plants in your house. You ask him to water and fertilize your orchids as well. A few days later, you notice that your orchids have started dying. You deduce that the cause was probably because orchids require a different type of fertilizer. Describe what may have happened in terms of your knowledge base, inference and memory on both your parts.

4.28 You want to learn something. Who is the best person to obtain knowledge from, and why?

4.29 You have a colleague who is vague when asked the basis of his decision. What do you do?

CHAPTER FIVE
THOSE BEAUTIFUL YOU'S

"Don't become your own enemy."

~ **Ian Breck**

You're absolutely fabulous! You're also here for a reason – you make the world a better place to be. Discover your purpose, pursue it, and enjoy the ride that living well provides! With life being such an amazing experience, I often wonder why so many people seem to squander the ultimate once-in-a-lifetime experience of life instead of becoming caught up in the drama of living. As it turns out, a chance meeting helped me answer this question.

I was at a gathering at Big Sur in California with several friends. I had just been introduced to Bob, a former finance executive who'd made the unexpected career leap to a French teacher only a few years earlier. As the night went on, we spoke often and would ultimately become friends. I was curious as to why he made such a radical career change when he was clearly at the top of his game in banking. He remarked that he was trained to be a banker, but born to be a teacher. At one point, the self-admitted Francophile posed an interesting question. "Tell me, Ian, when we're on our death beds, what will be our excuses for the dreams we never achieved because we were too busy living our lives?" Unfortunately, it took my own near death experience to understand the profundity of his question. C'est la vie.

Bob's question started thoughts whirring about why life's realities so often get in the way of living. As I considered that question again years later, I began questioning whether it was more about life getting in the way of our living – or perhaps it was us who get in the way of living our own lives.

Just a few years earlier, I had been involved in a project where we were attempting to understand more about why people appear to have two personas. I mean, why do we act one way when we're alone, and another when in the company of others? It's not a schizophrenia sort of thing. It's more of an instinctual/protective sort of thing. While differences between private and public personas are minimal for some, many people assume a very dissimilar persona in public. It's almost as if we have two "*self's*."

I spent untold hours exploring and hypothesizing. I spoke to psychologists and scientists - each of which had unique views, opinions, ideas, and thoughts on the subject. The more questions I asked, the more I developed - and the more intriguing the whole question of multiple personas became. There was something here - I just didn't know what.

With little or nothing to go on, I set out to create a model to help explain, or at least understand the dynamics of this peculiar behavior. The result of my efforts was the "*Two Self's Theory.*" This theory starts with an assumption that we use one of two distinct personas, or sets of behaviors, to interact with our world. This theory offers an interesting angle about what might be causing us to get in the way, or self-inhibit the experience of our own lives. It starts with our self, or "self's," as the case appears to be. Our two self's are closely related to each other, yet very different in terms of behavior and purpose.

Our first "self," or *true* self, is an exact reflection of our environment and life. It's all about us. It's defined by our loves, decisions, fears, successes, dreams, heartaches, losses, passions, failures, experiences, accomplishments, and everything about our lives. As a true reflection of us, our true self is always honest, realistic, and practical; after all, it's the "true" us. It's designed for realistic and pragmatic self-control; it grounds us.

Our second "self," our *idealized* self, is prettier, more debonair and affable than our more reticent true self. This is the self we display to the world – feathers and all. It's an exact copy of our true self, but with the addition of lipstick, eye shadow, a slit up the leg of the dress, and fishnet hose with a seam up the back. Our idealized self is designed for public consumption. It's not necessarily tied to any truth, reality, or practicality despite the fact it's derived from our true self. Then again, it doesn't have to be. It's a nimbler and more clever version of our true self that's designed for survival. It makes us approachable and reactive.

So, there you have it; one "self" for control, and another for survival. Like all human mechanisms, it's brilliant in its design. Nevertheless, what does all of this have to do with us getting in the way of living our lives better? To answer this question, we need to look a bit more closely at what's really happening.

You see, our "self's" are different by design. They do different jobs, despite being closely related. Regardless of any differences between the two, the ideal self is based on the real self. However, what happens when the idealized self goes haywire and tosses out the characteristics and features that it inherits from the true self and starts its own party of one? Or, what happens when the true self starts tossing bizarre characteristics at the ideal self? As it turns out, your "self's" don't always play well together. When this happens, they often wreak havoc on our lives.

Let's start by understanding what can happen with the true self. Because your true self encompasses everything about you, it's reflective of you. This means it expresses anything and everything about you and your life precisely. However, what happens when something disagreeable is introduced into your life like extreme stress, frustration, fear, or anxiety? That's right; these are reflected as well.

Your ideal self, on the other hand, has the luxury of tossing out what it doesn't want to share with the world – to a point. Your true self doesn't have that luxury; it reflects your reality precisely. So then, what are the limits of what your true self can handle in terms of stresses, turmoil and chaos? How long can your ideal self cover the realities of your true self without becoming strained itself? More importantly, when things get rough for your true self, do you tend to live your life more along the lines of our ideal self, which is more of a fantasy version of you? Or, do you align more closely with your true self and avoid interaction altogether, or express the frustration of your true self publicly?

Your idealized self, on the other hand, has its own very real set of problems. Although it's based on your true self, your ideal self is so responsive to its environment that it's influenced easily. Despite being designed for survival, it's not particularly limited to any certain script by its design. Is it possible that your idealized self could actually start believing that its survival behavior could become its reality, and ignore what it receives from the true self altogether? We've all been "caught up in the moment," and have done something entirely out of character at one time or another. Is such behavior really a case of our idealized self being influenced to a point that it enables us to break free of our reality and assume a different identity or persona other than our true self provides? And. if this can happen occasionally, what's to keep it from becoming an unending behavior? Can a leopard change its spots? The answer might surprise you.

These are interesting questions along with quite profound ramifications to explore. Of all we still don't understand, we do know that the results of such internal conflicts can result in or contribute significantly to anxiety, depression, and a host of other issues that can require professional intervention. They can also destroy life quality.

The distance between your two self's is called *"stratification."* When the distance between your two selfs is lower, you travel between them more easily in your daily life from a behavioral perspective. Your real self and true self are not that different from each other. In this case, your personal self is almost like your public self.

The result is that you are a more "real" person – which has significant benefits.

However, as the distance between our true and ideal self's increases, it becomes more difficult for us to jump between the two selfs behaviorally. This causes stresses that require more of our energy and focus to resolve and compensate for the differences between our real and idealized self's. In the end, such people are often very different in public than they are when at home. Extreme examples of this can often be observed with those in leadership positions and politics. They are super-human specimens in their public life, but are almost always far less in private. Transitioning between the two self's can cause problems that are devastating to life quality. It's kind of like an Elvis impersonator who can't quite get out his character once the gig is over. The result is often that a great deal of the pleasure of life and living is lost.

Unfortunately, our two self's don't always play well together. As humans, we tend to want to be seen, or at least perceived differently than what our true self suggests. After all, who wouldn't rather be seen as the happy-go-lucky, successful and well-respected person who everyone loves and admires instead of someone who snores, has bad breath, farts, and has scary bed head in the morning? This is where your idealized self comes into its element – it makes us more publicly acceptable.

In the real world, however, few of us are as extraordinary as our public behavior suggests. While your true self is too sterile, honest, and direct to get along well in the world, your idealized self talks the talk and walks the walk exceptionally well when it comes to interacting with your world. Your idealized self is so much more confident, and cooler than your more precise true self could ever be. However, when the differences between your true and ideal self's become too great, serious problems arise. Without a healthy balance and relationship between the two, your self's begin functioning as two separate and unrelated entities. From a quality of life perspective, it's like being married and having your illicit lover move in next door. It's doable, but the stress will most certainly kill the mood! Everyone experiences stratification to one degree or another in their lives – albeit hopefully sans the tryst!

Stratification works the other way as well. Having your self's too closely aligned can cause just as many problems as having them too far apart. Have you ever known someone who "blurts," or has no apparent filter between what they're thinking and when they say something? Have you ever known someone who acts inappropriately for a particular situation? These are examples of *inverse stratification* - two self's that are *too* closely aligned.

When it comes to living a high quality life, stratification is something you want to minimize at all costs - but it's not something you want or should expect to eliminate altogether. You need some distance between your two self's – just not too much.

The differences between your true and idealized self's are essential for survival. However, when the differences become too significant, problems set in quickly. It's essential to recognize the signs and intervene. When "heavy" stratification is present, you tend to feel it physiologically. Although everyone is different, some equate their feelings to "living two different lives," or "living a lie." If you have these sentiments, it's probably time to sit down and explore your life a bit more closely.

As distance between the true and ideal self's increase, so too do the number and strength of inhibitors to life quality. The idea is to minimize the distance between your two self's, but correcting stratification can be challenging. However, "keeping it real," to stratification is what "lose the weight" is to high blood pressure. It's simple and effective advice.

Keeping your idealized self "in balance" with your real self represents an important challenge of a quality life. Because our idealized self is so easily influenced, and is often more fun and gregarious than our true self would ever think of being, most people tend to wax poetic about living the life of their idealized self. And, who can blame them? On the other hand, when your idealized self becomes too far removed from your true self, you begin living a quite different reality that's almost impossible to maintain – at least for long.

The key to maintaining a healthy balance between your two self's is to protect what becomes a part of your life, and to ensure your ideals are practical, real, and don't override your reality - and ultimately how you live. In the end, a little balance goes a long way in helping you get out of the way of living and realizing all that life has to offer.

One of the most important exercises in a high quality life is aligning your true self as closely as possible to your idealized self without eliminating the distinctions of either. This mitigates the powerful and adverse influences stratification introduces to your life and its quality. Elevate your true self by building your life around those things that are important and valuable to you. Eliminate those things about your idealized self that are unreasonable, irrational, untrue, or not realistically attainable. This exercise will go a long way toward reducing stratification and the potentially catastrophic influences it introduces to your life.

When it comes to living a quality life, honesty about who you are makes you far more interesting, intriguing – and perfect in your own right. Keep the relationships between your self's healthy and balanced and ensure one is not inhibiting the other. Make sure the people surrounding you and your life experience the genuine wonderfulness only an engaging you has to offer – and not a false reflection of what you want them to see.

Where It Fits

Those with highly rewarding and satisfying lives often have self's that are more closely aligned than those with less satisfying lives.

You might be surprised to learn how few people realize their greatest detractor in life is themselves. This is a common revelation that virtually all High Q people I've known report in their journey to developing a happier and healthier life. It's also one of the first things I set out to discover about my clients.

The idea of keeping your self's "balanced" is about developing, creating, and maintaining a healthy perspective about who you really are. It's not always easy. However, it's an essential element of living well.

Practical Life Design Strategy

When thinking about what you have just read, and your life, please explore the following questions.

5.1 What constitutes your two "self's?"

5.2 Describe your "self's," and their purpose in your life.

5.3 If your "self's" are truly self-preservation mechanisms, what about them makes them protective?

5.4 What are the things that are different between your true self and your idealized self?

5.5 When thinking about the distance between your true and ideal self's (stratification), would you say that it's minimal, moderate, or extensive?

5.6 When thinking about your answer to the previous question, why?

5.7 Do you know someone who exhibits moderate or significant stratification? If so, what is the evidence that makes you think they are too highly stratified?

5.8 Do you know someone who exhibits moderate or significant stratification? If so, why do you think they are too stratified?

5.9 If you teach someone about stratification, what would you tell them?

5.10 Name three actions you can take to reduce the stratification in your own life today.

5.11 What are the risks or disadvantages of showing your true self to friends or others around you?

5.12 If you were to develop a strategy to minimize stratification in your own life, what would it look like?

CHAPTER SIX

INTRODUCING MOZART

"If life has to always be perfect for you to enjoy it, your life's strategy is flawed."

~ **Ian Breck**

You are truly intriguing. On one hand, you have the boisterous, street smart self that isn't necessarily tied to truth or justice - which makes it perfect for survival. Then you have its counterpart, which is nobler, always honest, and too goody-two-shoes for public consumption. You also have a knowledge-base, inference mechanism, free will, knowledge, and experience. An enormous collection of complex systems makes you possible. However, what is it within each of us that manages, or directs all of these resources to create our lives? (Cue sound effect: Creepy, ghostly, slide whistle music.)

As I began exploring more complex life issues, I came to a point where I couldn't help but wonder what brings together everything within us to provide direction and purpose in our lives – and how did, whatever that was, get what it needed or knows what it needs to influence and command our lives? I mean, what is it that makes us decide to go for a drive, have a baby, become a professor or a rock star, hold someone's hand, or kill? I already knew about knowledge, free will, and our two self's. However, none of those things really made any real sense without some omniscient controlling and organizing mother ship to put it all together. When I asked friends and colleagues their thoughts, I heard only crickets chirping. None had a plausible answer. I wanted to know more about what inside of us says, "Wake up! It's time to walk the dog," or "Oh - she just really didn't go there!" I wanted to know more about that little voice inside of my head.

This question haunted me for years. From the perspective of a knowledge geek like myself, this is the kind of thing that consumes your every waking moment – especially when you have no idea where to begin looking for the answers you need. After mentally wrangling this question ad nauseum for what seemed to be an eternity, I decided to journal my every thought and action for one week. I wasn't sure where it would lead, but it might reveal something interesting or at least useful along the way – and possibly even a place to begin my search for answers.

Let me begin by telling you that, until my experiment, I used to think people who listened to voices in their heads were either psychopaths or axe murderers. However, after asking around a bit, I discovered each of us has an "*inner voice*" that guides us toward what is important in life; and to warn us when something isn't quite right. As it turns out, that inner voice is the tip of a much larger and even more profound iceberg.

Within each of us exists a "conductor" of sorts. Your conductor's sole purpose is to direct you through each day of your life – and protect you. Some people call it their guardian angel, conscience, or more simply, that voice in their head. I named my life conductor "*Mozart*."

So, what is Mozart all about? Your inner conductor is the director of your life. It points you in the direction of your interests and passions while providing an invaluable first line of reason-based defense against hazards you might encounter. It does its job by gathering absolutely everything about you from your knowledge and expertise to your personal history and experiences. A remarkable process then occurs where, in mere milliseconds, your knowledge and rules to environmental considerations and previous experiences are gathered to direct every move you make and ultimately becomes the lens through which you interact with your world. You're probably more familiar with your conductor as "that little voice inside my head." Because it exists somewhere between your physical and idealized self, most scientists aren't really sure what to make of it.

To be formally introduced to your inner Mozart, locate a pen after you read this paragraph. At the very second you recognize a pen, notice the voice in your head that tells you, "That's a pen." Before you locate a pen, however, you will also locate other things for which you will hear something like, "that's a pencil," or "that's a telephone." It happens just that quickly and you might not notice it unless you pay closer attention, but you'll eventually hear it. This is your inner Mozart at work. It's a remarkable dialogue where your mind interacts with your brain, body, and your environment in terms each understands. Your inner Mozart is the master translator between the language of your body, mind, and the world.

How does Mozart accomplish all of these astonishing feats? After all, it's one thing to recall knowledge, it's a quantum leap, however, to leverage that knowledge and initiate actions based on it – and in real time. Although we certainly don't understand Mozart to any truly discernible degree, I tell my clients that Mozart is really a smarter version of both your true and ideal self's - just without all of the external pressures. Mozart isn't afraid to take chances and push you to live your life more completely, unlike your true self that is uber-cautious and probably too honest, careful, and self-protective. Your true self is often so careful about protecting you, that if it were allowed to conduct your life, you'd be wearing a hardhat to birthday parties!

Why do we need a Mozart anyway? Mozart is the inner coordinator of your life; your personal mother ship. Others see Mozart quite differently. Remember Renee Descartes of dualism and ten ways to piss off the Catholic Church fame? He believed the *pineal gland*, a tiny gland tucked neatly between the two hemispheres of the brain (also known as the "third eye"), was "the seat of the soul" that controls our lives. The pineal gland was where Descartes' believed his Mozart lived – which became his ultimate undoing as far as the Church was concerned.

Mozart uses your knowledge, experience, and input from the world around you to direct your actions and enable you to interact with your environment. So, how does it all work together – and why should you care? If Mozart does exist, where does it get the knowledge it needs to know what it does about you and your life? Your inner Mozart relies on a pre-defined set of underlying rules and logic to do its job. These are referred to as *core strategies*. Here is where the story of you becomes truly fascinating.

So, what's the big deal about conductors, the inner you, and things like core strategies? It's simple: when it comes to how you live your life, your core strategy provides the underlying rules and instructions you use to live your life. Just as the greatest designs are based on an overall vision, your core strategy provides the strategic blueprint for how you live your life. It doesn't provide the specifics, however. It only provides your life's general underlying logic. As you are about to learn, this is indeed significant.

As I began learning more about inner Mozarts, frameworks, and core strategies, I wanted to understand how they genuinely influenced life. I mean, when life's going well, it's apparent that Mozart and the core strategy it relies upon are playing well together. They're said to be "in harmony." However, what occurs when that harmony becomes compromised or is unable to keep up in some way? As it turns out, a compromised core strategy can have a devastating impact on life and its quality.

How well your core strategy keeps up with the realities of your life determines how well your life works for you. When your core strategy and reality are at odds, the consequences can be deadly. For growing numbers of people whose core strategies are feeling the strain of lives in turmoil, the resulting stress and anxiety of everyday living is contributing to record levels of disease, divorce, violence, financial destruction, psychological disorders, and dysfunction. As it turns out, the core strategies that drive our lives and our realities are exceptionally interwoven.

Like most humans, Mozart needs to know it's doing well. When Mozart believes it's not performing satisfactorily, it begins an instinctual search for new strategies capable of meeting the changing demands of living. As it turns out, Mozart is very serious about meeting our needs. When it reaches or exceeds its design limits, it gets nervous and responds accordingly.

So, is it possible that the reality of life and living can stress the design of our core strategies? Statistics offer grim reminders that we may be reaching the theoretical limits of our strategic design. Despite America being rated highly in terms of our standard of living – (which is falling more rapidly than at any other time in recorded history), numerous reports describe upwards of 85% of all American's reporting rapidly increasing dissatisfaction with the quality of their lives. One in five Americans now receives food stamp benefits, and one in every five homes is underwater and/or delinquent on its mortgage. Perhaps the most alarming statistic of all is that an estimated 8 million American's now consider suicide each year. Suicide is now the tenth leading cause of death in America according to the most recent United States Centers for Disease Control death statistics data for 2009.

When it comes to life and living, there may be far more than meets the eye when it comes to the performance and importance of our core strategies.

Strategically Speaking

When we watch a golf game, we're witnessing strategies playing out in real time. Solutions are created based on experience. Decisions are tested against expertise. Problems are solved using both. Some players focus on defense. For others, it's all about offense.

The rest fall somewhere in between. Life is much the same with regard to how we live it - it's all about strategy!

To give direction to your life, your inner Mozart relies on your core strategy to do a great deal of its heavy lifting. Your core strategy provides overall direction, general instructions, and the rules you use to live your life. Thankfully, we don't have to worry about managing a huge number of core strategies. As humans, our core strategies are predominantly grouped into one of two particular styles. The *synthetic core strategy* is used by most individuals. It's all about goals. It's simple and tidy as far as strategies go. We simply define goals and achieve them. Much less used, but highly venerated and exploited by those who live high quality lives, is the *organic core strategy*. This strategy challenges us to design and create an environment where outcomes emerge naturally. The differences between these two are profoundly significant, both in terms of how they work and the lifestyles they produce.

So, which core strategy is better? Each has advantages and disadvantages. Let's take a closer look.

THE SYNTHETIC STRATEGY

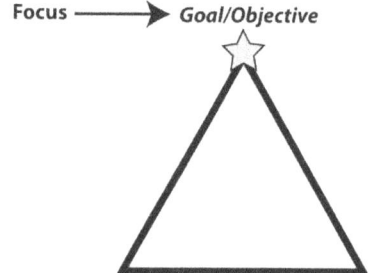

The *synthetic core strategy* is the most common core strategy used today. Synthetic strategies are easy, measurable, and predictable – they're all about goals. With a synthetic strategy driving your life, it becomes a series of objectives to be achieved. Get the education, marry the spouse, buy the house, have the kids, and so on. Check. Check. Check. The synthetic core strategy makes perfect sense for those who prefer a more task-based existence – and there are many. It's efficient, simple, repeatable, measurable, predictable, and can be applied effortlessly as you meander throughout your day without a great deal of thought. People who employ this as their primary core strategy are referred to as *synthetic people*.

The synthetic strategy is quite simple and requires only that you establish a goal, and then do whatever is required to achieve that goal. It's tidy and easily understandable as far as strategies go. It also offers some semblance of control, which is an important added benefit to many today who don't typically experience a great amount of control in their own lives. This feature alone, albeit more pseudo than actual, makes the synthetic core strategy even more attractive.

As wonderfully simplistic and efficient as the synthetic strategy appears at first, it also has its dark side. All too often, achieving goals and objectives becomes the driving focus for those who consider achievement a valid metric of self-worth and success.

When achieving goals that either you or others have established for you, all is well within your world. However, when your ability to achieve those objectives is compromised, many of your feelings of well-being, confidence, and self-satisfaction related to you and your quality of life deteriorate rapidly. You're only as good as your last victory. Unemployment, poor health, and unforeseeable problems not only adversely affect synthetic core strategic performance, but also the individual and their sense of wellbeing profoundly. In the end, the synthetic strategy is fine – until you lose your capacity to feed it.

The synthetic strategy certainly has its place in our lives. However, that place must be tempered with a healthy dose of "Plan B." Let's take a closer look at the potential perils of the synthetic strategy.

I had a friend who wanted to build a new home several years ago. I learned he intended to build his home using an interest-only loan. When he informed me of his decision, I questioned his reasoning. He told me that, had he selected a conventional loan, his payments would have been unaffordable. I suggested he consider waiting until such a time when he had saved a bit more and could afford a conventional loan. His response was predictable. "If I don't build it now, I never will."

My friend's logic had obvious and serious flaws from the onset – unless, of course, you were him. For starters, he ignored his obviously less-than-favorable financial realty. Instead of listening to that little voice in his head, he sought to override it by reinforcing his flawed decision logic in other ways. His knowledge base was intact and complete. He acknowledged the risks. He moved ahead anyway. Where was Mozart – and what was he thinking?

Unfortunately, his flawed pursuit found a willing partner in a synthetic core strategy that made achieving a goal, however misdirected, more valuable than the possibility of jeopardizing he and his family's future. It was the ultimate roll of the dice. Unfortunately, the additional reinforcement he sought was readily available from mortgage brokers and bankers who ignored his precarious finances, lack of sophistication, and misguided desire to originate a loan. By seeking additional reinforcement to a poor decision, he was also creating potential sources of blame if his life failed to pan out as he hoped.

This scenario ultimately introduced my friend to a very new and poignant reality. My friend's goal of building a new home had become such a driving force in his life, that "cheap" money, the "American dream," and self-serving bankers reinforced his myopic focus and reckless vision. He wasn't looking for rational thinking - he was seeking reasons to justify poor judgment and risky decisions. To date, he has almost lost his home at least twice, and finds himself in a constant struggle to stay on top of his bills. He recently entered a credit program to keep his home at the cost of his credit – and more than $7,000 in upfront costs. In the end, his decision to achieve a particular goal proved to be the Trojan horse that has all but destroyed him, his family, and their quality of life. It happens just this easily.

Unfortunately, my friend is not unique. He is one of tens of millions of Americans facing the same reality today. The only exception being that for others it can be anything from advertising to social pressure that puts them over the edge. If you're thinking this represents a minority of Americans, think again. In 2011, 28.4 million of an estimated 130 million homes in America were under water – that's about one in every five homes. More than 55 percent of all single-family homes with a mortgage in Atlanta, 50% of all homes in Florida, and more than 68 percent of all single-family homes with a mortgage in Phoenix are underwater. Thirteen percent of all American homes now sit vacant. In 2011, new home sales in America were down 80% from their peak in July 2005. Foreclosure filings in the United States are projected to increase by another 20 percent in 2011-2012. In September 2008, 33 percent of Americans knew someone who had been foreclosed upon or who was facing eminent foreclosure. By 2011, that number had risen to 48 percent. This illustrates a systemic consumer crisis and an incontrovertible indicator of the struggling strategies of individuals, culture, and society. Most importantly, this is a sobering reminder of the potential volatility of goal-centric synthetic strategies both on personal and social levels.

For my friend, it was a house, credit, the American dream, misdirected goals and a corrupted life strategy that drove the series of poor decisions that precipitated his fall from grace. For others, it might be health, credit, debt, or the loss of a job that triggers the fall. Regardless of the reason, this same scenario is played out in the lives of millions of individuals every day.

Despite the potential perils, the synthetic strategy remains the most common life strategy employed today. It provides order, predictability, reproducibility, measurability, and a straightforward approach for organizing life. However, most people are simply unaware of other alternatives.

THE ORGANIC STRATEGY

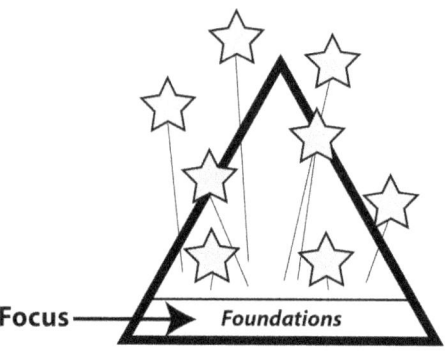

People who live high quality lives are indeed different from the rest. This difference isn't just behavioral - it's organic. High Q people tend to follow a very different core strategy than most. They follow an *organic core strategy*. We call such individuals *organic people*.

The organic core strategy stands apart from its synthetic counterpart in one spectacular way - its focus is not on goals and objectives. In fact, it's almost anti-goal! The focus of the organic strategy is on creating an environment where a quality life can emerge and flourish on its own. Think of the organic strategy as a vineyard. Your focus isn't on the grapes as much as the soil. You want your soils healthy and able to provide what fantastic grapes require to grow and flourish!

Unlike the synthetic strategy that sees life as a goal-centric exercise, an organic strategy rewards interaction and preparation. I tell my clients an organic strategy is all about riding the wave of life.

Fill your life with all you are passionate about, and then be prepared to follow where it takes you. In other words, be the grape!

So, what does an organic core strategy look like in real life? It's deceptively simple - the key word being *deceptively*. In its most basic sense, the organic core strategy focuses on creating the foundation for a wonderful life based on those things you're most passionate about, and allowing that foundation to grow a life that will flourish. It's like the Japanese art of flower arranging, *ikebana*. It's not about the flower itself, but the leaves, stalks, and the plant in its totality that become the focus of the designer. From a design perspective, it's ultimately about the space between each stem that matters most. If you want another perspective, think of architecture. Fine architecture is not about the structure itself. It's the space that remains that ultimately defines the brilliance of its design. The organic life is very much the same in a philosophical and structural sense.

The beauty of the organic core strategy is that it's about the experience of life and living. Someone with a love of photography is a great example. Whereas a synthetic person may see photography as a series of technological challenges to be mastered, the organic individual sees photography as an opportunity to explore and share his or her world and observe it from different viewpoints, a creative outlet, and an opportunity to be with friends, and possibly even make it a career. With synthetic people, it's definitely more about the destination. Organic people focus far more intently on the journey.

Organic people are unique in other ways as well. In addition to lives designed around their passions, they are far more likely to transform their passions into careers. The attorney who becomes a baker, or the manager who becomes an actor are common examples of organic core strategies at work. Organic people are intensely aware of their lives and relish sharing their story. If you know someone who is a High Q person, ask about his or her life.

You'll usually hear a story of fascinating transformation that you can use as inspiration to reimagine your own life.

Activity and interaction are the currencies of organic people and their lives. They crave "doing" what they love whether it is a simple garden or something as grandiose as designing a skyscraper. Organic individuals don't simply live life - they love it!

By this point, you're probably thinking how great it would be to live an organic life – but you still have to pay your bills! Organic people are no different. The primary difference is that organic people tend to design their lives around what's important to them, and adjust their realities to facilitate their ideal life experiences.

At first glance, the organic strategy appears to be somewhat arbitrary and random in terms of outcome. I've found quite the opposite to be true. Organic strategies benefit from both chance and the prepared mind. Unlike synthetic strategies that require goal chasing, organic core strategies require people to be more creative with their lives, dream, create a vision, and be willing to let life take them where it may. With adequate preparation, the results of an organic strategy will always exceed those of synthetic strategies in terms of both personal satisfaction and quality of life. Perhaps this is why virtually all people who live truly high quality lives exhibit strong organic characteristics in the design of their lives.

The organic strategy also provides an interesting side benefit. Because it's so focused on the interests of the individual as opposed to the masses, it tends to insulate individuals from many of the stresses that life presents. Although unsure of all of the reasons why this occurs, I personally believe being more protective of their lifestyle and interests, and a built in support system are influential contributing factors.

One point worth mentioning is that organic people are generally much more deliberate about their lives than are synthetic people – sometimes to a point of appearing indifferent or arrogant. Don't misread this. Organic people know what they want from life, and are highly disinclined to make compromises.

Another intriguing characteristic of organic people is that they derive deep pleasure from the more esoteric features of life and the world around them. The beauty and scent of flowers, the exploration of exceptional food, classic jazz on the beach with friends, interaction with others and even the story behind a great film are highly valued rudiments of their lives. These are only a few of the things that make them so interesting and engaging. It's difficult to have a bad time when an organic individual is in the room!

So, are there problems with the organic strategy? As with the synthetic strategy, it's not so much about problems with the strategy itself as it is with those who employ it. The most significant issue my clients experience when transitioning to a more organic strategy is that of creativity and knowing what to do next. Because most have lived synthetic lives firmly rooted in achieving goals and objectives, many find it exceptionally difficult to transition to a more organic strategy. The organic strategy is not difficult, but does require you to build upon those things that are important to you, then allow your life to "happen" from that point onward. That's quite a bit of trust for a goal-getter to brandish! This can be a stretch for some people – and professional assistance or mentorship can make a profound difference in this area.

In Conclusion

The experience and the ultimate quality of our lives are influenced significantly by the core strategy we adopt. And yes, it's a choice we all make. A synthetic strategy deeply roots life quality in your ability to achieve goals. An organic life strategy defines the quality of your life by your ability to create an environment where life can flourish. The choice is yours as to which you pursue.

It's very important to understand that core strategies are mutually exclusive and cannot be expressed in terms of a polar scale. It's not like you have the synthetic strategy on one end of the scale and an organic strategy on the other and you fall somewhere between the two. That's not how it works as there are no direct correlations between the two strategies. You can, however, use one strategy for some activities, and the second one for others. The strategic approach that dominates your life is the strategy that ultimately describes you.

Just because you're predominately synthetic doesn't mean you can or won't switch teams from time to time. Most of us dream about retiring to a completely organic lifestyle devoid of meetings, goals, and pressures from our synthetic pasts. While you never completely eliminate all synthetic elements from your life, you can significantly reduce them, or at least use them in more select applications.

Where It Fits

When you go to college, you choose a major that defines your curriculum, and probably your career – at least for a while. (Statistics tell us you'll change careers about seven times in your life.) Life strategies are very similar with the exception that we tend to "favor" one strategy over the other based on which ones are most familiar with, and are comfortable using.

Life strategies provide the base strategic foundation for how you live your life. Most people migrate toward the synthetic task-based strategy because that's what they're most familiar with. High Q people, on the other hand, migrate toward a more organic, or experiential strategy. The differences between the two are quite profound. Can you experience a high quality life using a synthetic strategy? Yes you can – but there are significantly greater challenges and adversities you will encounter due to the nature of the strategy. A overwhelming majority of all people who live deeply satisfying quality lives employ an organic core strategy.

In the end, however, the choice is yours. Understanding each strategy and its strengths and weaknesses allows you to live your life using a core strategy that best suits your personality and desired lifestyle.

Practical Life Design Strategy

When thinking about what you have just read, and your life, please consider the following questions.

6.1 What is the function and purpose of "that little voice" in your head?

6.2 What is the purpose of your inner you?

6.3 What role does your core strategy play in your life?

6.4 How is a core strategy developed?

6.5 Are you a synthetic or organic person?

6.6 Do you live a synthetic or organic lifestyle?

6.7 If 6.5 and 6.6 are different, what impact does this have on your life?

6.8 Looking at question 6.5, why are you not the other type of strategy?

6.9 What are your perceptions of the synthetic core strategy?

6.10 What are your perceptions of the synthetic core lifestyle?

6.11 What are your perceptions of the organic core strategy?

6.12 What are your perceptions of the organic lifestyle?

6.13 When thinking about your core strategy and life, describe your life in terms of the core strategy you most closely follow.

6.14 Considering your answer to question 6.13, which core strategy would you prefer to drive your life and why?

6.15 If you could change anything about your life and strategy, what would it be?

6.16 We talked about a synthetic core strategy being about the destination and the organic core strategy being about the journey. Describe what I meant by this statement.

6.17 Thinking about core strategies, which one are we all born with and why?

6.18 Can a core strategy ever change in life - and why?

6.19 What would it require to change a core strategy in your life?

6.20 What event would it take you to change your core strategy and why?

6.21 Name 5 people who employ synthetic strategies – and how you can tell they use the strategy they do.

6.22 Name 5 people who employ organic strategies – and how you can tell they use the strategy they do.

CHAPTER SEVEN
DECISIONS. DECISIONS.

"The quality of your life is a direct reflection of the quality of your decisions."

~ **Ian Breck**

Decisions. We make literally thousands of them each day. Some are so very minute and seemingly inconsequential that they've become instinctual. Others have the potential to alter life. With all of our decision-making experience, you would think we would be exceptional decision-makers in our own right. Unfortunately, decision-making isn't our strong suit. Few people have any real idea about what drives the decisions they make despite making from 40,000 to 100,000 of them each day. Part of this is because most of the decisions we make have become so automatic or embedded in our behaviors that we seldom realize we're making them when we do.

While effective decisions certainly aren't the exclusive domain of High Q people, they tend to possess a remarkably high-level command of decision-making. When it comes to living well, most experts believe the single greatest determinant of life quality is the ability to arrive at effective decisions. Because you're a product of your decisions, smarter decision-making is an essential life quality skill.

So, what is a decision? Actually, "making a decision" is a term we use to explain the entire process of determining the best possible choice from a list of potential choices we've developed. It's important to understand what's actually happening.

Decision-making skills, or more accurately, our lack of them, are most people's dirty little secret. Few truly understand the details of effective decision-making, or what constitutes a "good" decision.

Despite making literally thousands of them each day, the average person is woefully inept when it comes to understanding how they make the decisions they make – and it often shows in the quality of their lives. The reason? We are simply never taught this rudimentary life activity in school.

In its most basic sense, every decision is a problem to be solved - at least that's how your brain sees it. If you have a question to answer, a decision to arrive at, a solution to create, or a problem to solve, your brain sees all of these as problems to be solved. Moreover, when your brain sees a problem that needs to be solved, it automatically begins an exhaustive search for possible or plausible solutions.

Making an accurate decision isn't difficult. However, understanding how the decision-making process works and the different strategies that can be employed increases the effectiveness and accuracy of decisions significantly.

A decision's "answer" is actually the result of a three-step process of understanding the problem, gathering the best choices, and selecting the best available one for the situation.

Step 1: Understanding the Question/Problem

One of the most common problems associated with decision-making has more to do with the problem itself rather than the decision. In all too many cases, the problem we're trying to solve is not clearly defined or understood. We've all been guilty of this gaffe, and it can be quite embarrassing when it occurs. However, despite being one of the most common reasons for poor decisions, this faux pas is simple to remedy: make sure that you're answering the appropriate question! Verify your understanding of the problem by concurring with others before going any further.

Step 2: Developing the Best Choices

The best decision makers admit to a majority of their time being spent exploring and developing choices. Developing choices is a critical element of the decision-making process because the quality of your choices determines the ultimate quality of your decision. If you have inferior choices, your decision will reflect the quality of those choices. Great choices, on the other hand, take decisions to new heights and inspire discussion, interaction, and innovation. This is where "thinking outside the box" comes into play. Perhaps the most important advice I can offer about potential decision choices is that you can rarely have too many of them. Choices that don't fit well will be sorted out later in the final selection process.

Developing choices is an art to survey experts. Professionals who design and develop research surveys are masters of question and choice design. The common problem most pros admit to is that their questions are often so finely crafted that respondents tend to choose the best answer in their minds before they finish reading the actual question itself!

Thankfully, most of us are not quite so research-oriented and tend to develop our options based on "reasonable" choices we can think of quickly. This is referred to as *"ad-hoc"* choice development. Unfortunately, quickly created choices are rarely good ones. There are better ways of discovering the best possible choices when time permits.

A more powerful strategy for developing choices is to bring together a group of experts and explore the possible choices to be included in any particular decision. This strategy is called *collective development*, and it's a great place to begin when you have the time and semantic knowledge available. The trick to this approach is to understand your decision strategy before starting the process. We'll explore decision strategies in a moment.

So, how do master decision makers develop the choices for their decisions in real life? They tend to use a hybrid approach that combines collective development and decision point strategies, which we will explore in the next section. You already use many of these strategies to some degree, but probably not in any formalized or predictive manner.

Step 3: The Decision Point: Determining the Best Choice

When it comes to making a great decision, it's judgment that ultimately leads you to the final choice. Unfortunately, not everyone has great judgment. This is where the decision process most commonly breaks down. The good news is that most human decision-making relies on one of six strategies. Understanding these strategies is easy, provides built-in judgment for the most part, and adds far greater accuracy to your decisions. Let's take a closer look at the strategic options.

The "Superior" Strategy

This strategy states that if you have two choices, you explore the details of each. If choice 1 has at least one attribute more attractive than choice 2, and the remaining attributes are the same, then choice 1 is selected.

Let's go shopping for cars to explore an example of the superior strategy. You have found two gorgeous Ferrari 458 Spiders that look absolutely fabulous on you! The problem is you only have about $300k on you and can only purchase one while you're out and about! Both cars are identical except that one is red, and the other is black. Which one do you buy and why? In this case, you select the red one because the color is more attractive to you, and all other features of the cars are equal. In this case, color becomes the differentiating, or *salient*, feature that drives your decision.

The superior strategy makes short work of decision-making. Perhaps that's why it's so often overused and misapplied. The superior strategy, or some variation of it, has become the de facto decision-making strategy for many people today. While extremely efficient, it is rarely the best strategy because it's not particularly in-depth in terms of reasoning, and offers virtually nothing in terms of choice development. Before applying the superior strategy to your decisions, understand its nature, and ensure that it's the best strategy for your particular decision. In most cases, other strategies are often better choices.

The "One Bad All Bad" Strategy

The One Bad All Bad strategy requires that you establish the features each possible choice must possess before it is considered a potential choice. If any choice does not have even one of the features specified, that choice is removed from consideration.

To understand this strategy, let's go shopping - again! (Gee, you sure must really like to shop!) You have another cat-thing. It's growing, but it's not quite ready to leave the house and go to college. Nevertheless, it needs a house that it can call its own – other than your five closest neighbors. You decide your cat's perfect house must have a swinging door, a light, a built-in food dispenser, carpet, a sushi and water tray, and a window. Cat-things are so demanding!

You go to the pet store and tell the salesperson you want a cathouse. After the slight misunderstanding and the ensuing scuffle with store security has ended, you begin looking at cathouses. If a cathouse doesn't possess even just one of the features you specified, it is removed from consideration.

This strategy has many benefits, but is also a rather cut and dried proposition as it leaves no room for compromise. However, it can be used until compromise is required. Let's assume that no cathouses in the store meet your criteria. You could then move to another strategy and determine which cathouses most closely meet those criteria. That being said, this is an exceptional strategy to develop choices for decisions when you have a minimum set of criteria, and Plan B options for if or when this strategy fails.

The "At Least" Strategy

As with the One Bad All Bad strategy, the At Least strategy requires that you select a set of features for each choice you want to include for consideration. The difference is that before you include a choice for consideration, that choice's most important features must exceed your minimum specifications.

To understand the At Least strategy better, let's head off to the electronics store. (Shopping again? Get help before it's too late!) You are interested in purchasing a new television this time. You want a television that has *at least* a 42" LCD screen, along with *at least* 2 HDMI plugs, *at least* a 120Hz screen refresh rate and it *must be* high definition. Each television you find that meets or exceeds your minimum criteria will be included in your list of possible choices for your final decision.

The At Least strategy is an exceptional strategy for selecting and evaluating choices when either a few or many minimum criteria must be met before a choice can be included in the potential choice list. This is also a wonderful strategy for reducing large numbers of possible choices to a smaller, more manageable selection - providing you know your selection criteria.

The "Attractiveness" Strategy

The Attractiveness strategy is an interesting strategy where you explore several possible choices and arrange their features in order of importance. Once you have ordered every feature of every choice, you then explore the top features of the possible choices and determine which choice is the most attractive to you. This is an excellent strategy for determining which choice is best for you.

To understand this strategy better, usher in the politicians! You are not sure about whom you will be voting for in the upcoming election. You explore the issues and positions of each candidate. You create a list for each candidate and list his or her positions on the issues in order of their importance to you. Once complete, you review the top five or so issues from each candidate and decide on one whose positions on the top five issues are most attractive to you.

If you are unsure of the features your choices should possess, this is the strategy for you! In this case, you order the features of each potential choice in order of their importance to you. Once you have them ordered, you simply compare and contrast each to see which features are most attractive to you. Your choices become the potential choices for the best possible candidates for you.

This is an exceptional strategy when you do not know something, and want to identify the most important features of any potential choice.

The "Elimination" Strategy

The Elimination strategy combines elements from the One Bad All Bad and the Attractiveness strategies to form a hybrid approach.

The Elimination strategy requires first that you establish the criteria for the features that are essential to the choices you ultimately select – just like in the One Bad All Bad strategy. Once your essential features have been defined, temporarily set your One Bad All Bad features list aside.

The next step in this process requires you to list the features of each possible choice by order of importance, as with the Attractiveness strategy.

Next, we compare the ranked features of each potential choice to the required feature list of the One Bad-All Bad features list we created in the first step. If any feature does not meet or exceed what was defined in the One Bad-All Bad features list, that choice is removed from consideration. This is repeated for all possible options. It sounds complicated, but it's not once you explore an example.

Let's look for a hotel to understand this strategy better.

You are taking your family on vacation and want to find the best possible hotel (probably because you are tired of shopping). Your first and most important criterion is that the hotel must be close to a ski area. Your next most important criterion is that it has an indoor pool and an onsite restaurant.

In this case, all hotels that are not in the proximity of a ski area, have no indoor pool and no restaurant are dropped from consideration immediately thanks to the One Bad All Bad strategy. The features of the remaining hotels are then listed in order of their importance to you. The hotels with the most attractive top features are then placed in consideration for your decision.

This decision strategy is great for whittling down many potential choices based on one or more major elimination criteria. It then allows you to determine the best potential choices based on criteria you may or may not necessarily know. In other words, this strategy is great for "I don't know what I want exactly, but my final choice must meet this or that criteria" type of situations.

The "Total Score" Strategy

The Total Score strategy is used to determine the "best" possible choice based on values assigned to a choice's features. It's easy: the choice with the highest score wins!

For an example of this strategy, let's look to an employment scenario. As one of the world's premier kitchen blender guru's, you are being courted by three companies who want you as their new kitchen blender shopping star! However, you are unsure which company has the best offer for you. To decide, you create three columns on a sheet of paper. Each column represents a company and each line contains an element of their job offer such as company-paid insurance, two-to-one 401k matching, salary, etc. Based on your perceived value of each feature of your offers, you assign a score. The scoring can be as simple as 1's and 0's for yes and no, to more sophisticated weighted, averaged numbering or stochastic schemes if you happen to be a completely nerded-out math geek! The choice is up to you as long as the same scoring system is used throughout the process – and you can keep up with the math!

Once you have assigned all elements of every offer a value, you simply tally the scores from each offer to arrive at your "best" choice.

Think a bit before using this strategy. Experts are cautious about the effectiveness and implementation of this strategy because of its subjectivity and significant opportunity for inaccuracy. As far as I am concerned, I consider this a potentially flawed strategy and avoid it like the plague – however, I have used it in the past for quick and dirty decisions. Nonetheless, many people use this strategy in their decisions - especially when they are unsure as to the best decision strategy to use. Some experts find this strategy useful to "rough in," or make quick predictions of the potential results of a decision.

In Conclusion

The first activity when making any decision of significance should be deciding the most appropriate strategy to be employed. From that point, great decisions rely on developing the pool of best possible choices according to your strategy, and finally employing decision strategies that yield the best possible outcomes. If you want to test your decision, try using more than one decision strategy and see if your answer is the same. Accurate answers most often are.

An imperative of the decision-making process is making your decision logic publicly available. Never miss an opportunity to sit down with others and explore the problem, potential choices, and the logic that drives your decision before you adopt it. If your thinking is wrong or incomplete, input from others goes far toward eliminating embarrassing and potentially costly mistakes. If your thinking is accurate, others will learn from your thought processes, insight, and expertise while the entire community benefits from the interaction and exchange. Either way, your energy can be focused on a solution while covering your bases at that same time!

Validation is essential. When it comes to decisions, each must be able to be validated - it must stand up to or shut down scrutiny.

If you don't already have it, embrace the challenge! If you've arrived at your decision accurately, describing the problem, the potential solutions, and explaining your strategy will make you look like the true genius you really are! Don't be afraid to demand this from others around you as well.

Effective decision-making requires a bit of practice. However, the resulting decisions are far more accurate, concise, and have the potential to change your life profoundly!

Where It Fits

Decisions are the most common and demanding mental activity you will undertake on any given day. They are also the most improperly applied and abused feature of knowledge and expertise. Because of the remarkable importance and influence that decisions impart on your life and its quality, effective decision-making is an essential skill in a high quality life.

Poor quality decisions associated with decision-making, solution creation, and problem solving represent the single greatest inhibitors to life quality. In a study conducted by River Bend Research in 2000, it was determined the median four-year American university business school graduate demonstrated less than 4% accuracy in their critical decision-making capabilities. By simply understanding basic decision types, and applying them appropriately, decision-making, problem solving, and solution-creation accuracy increased by a stunning average of more than 885%!

Practical Life Design Strategy

When thinking about what you have just read, and your life, please explore the following questions.

7.1 What is a decision?

7.2 What are the three primary activities of the decision-making process?

7.3 Name three issues that can cause problems when it comes to arriving at a decision.

7.4 When it comes to choices for your decision, what is the worst way to arrive at the possible choices in most cases – and why?

7.5 When it comes to choices for your decision, what are at least three of the most important things to keep in mind?

7.6 Why are decisions the single greatest determinant of our quality of life?

7.7 What are the six primary decision strategies?

7.8 You are looking to purchase a new watch. You are unsure of the watch and the features you are looking for. What do you do?

7.9 You are looking for a new home. Nothing quite meets your expectations. How do you determine the best overall home in this group?

7.10 Your friends are looking to adopt a child. They want a baby girl only. What are the potential downfalls with their thinking?

7.11 Your boss wants you to solve a problem and gives you a list of three possible solutions. He also suggests one that he prefers. You learn that his suggestion is not the best possible choice.

How did you discover this - and how do you approach your boss?

7.12 Your friend makes a decision that results in unintended consequences. What could have gone wrong?

7.13 You are looking for a hotel. It has to be close to a ski area. You would also prefer an indoor pool and an onsite restaurant. You eliminate all of the hotels that are not in the proximity of ski areas. However, all of the remaining hotels have indoor pools and onsite restaurants. Now what?

7.14 Which strategy(s) should you use if you have no idea about the features of the best possible choices?

7.15 You are looking to buy a car. You know that you want at least 32MPG, and a minimum of 300 horsepower. Which decision strategy do you use?

7.16 You have to make a decision and have developed all of your choices. You want an estimate of what the potential outcome of a decision might be. How do you do this?

7.17 Name three situations where a Superior decision strategy can be applied properly.

7.18 Name three situations where a One Bad All Bad decision strategy can be applied properly.

7.19 Name three situations where an At Least decision strategy can be applied properly.

7.20 Name three situations where an Attractiveness decision strategy can be applied properly.

7.21 Name three situations where an Elimination decision strategy can be applied properly.

7.22 Name three situations where a Total Score decision strategy can be applied properly.

7.23 You make a decision and discover that your choice was wrong. How could this happen?

7.24 What can you do to ensure you have accurate and complete knowledge before arriving at any decision?

7.25 Name five reasons why decision validation is important?

CHAPTER EIGHT
LIFE QUALITIES

"A quality life is not so much about all you have. It's almost more about what you don't."

~ **Ian Breck**

By this point in the game, you're probably asking yourself what "life quality" really is. In fact, you're probably also curious about what a "quality life" is. Is it about exotic cars, mansions, unusual European butterfly-antennae spa treatments, or perhaps traveling the world on your own private jet? Life qualities could also be something more esoteric like floating down a creek on inner tubes, a day at the beach, or making love. Is a quality life the stuff of the wealthy and socially privileged? Is it exclusive or inclusive? Is it something anyone can have or something only the few will ever possess? I found myself asking these very questions over twenty years ago. When talking about a quality life these days, there seem to be as many questions as people longing for the experience. My mistake was thinking there was a single definitive answer to what a quality life is. There isn't.

So, what really is a "quality" life? Life is a quantitative thing - each of us has one. A high quality life, on the other hand, is *qualitative* – it has specific qualities that make it different from an ordinary life. Therefore, a "high quality" life has absolutely nothing to do with material objects. Toss out your ideas of jets, champagne, or that mansion on the hill. While you're at it, rid yourself of any notions of it having anything to do with how much money you have, whom you know, or the size of your corner office. For many, these things more often inhibit the ability to experience a high quality life rather than contribute to it.

The qualities of your life are found in the *emotional responses* you experience from living your life. This is what I mean when I say, "*Activity is the currency of life.*" The emotional responses associated with the activities in your life contribute to your senses of satisfaction, self-esteem, contentment, reward, love, well-being, and a host of other emotions that influence who you are as a person and how you feel about yourself and your sense of wellbeing. If your sense of wellbeing is nourished with positive and affirming emotions, you experience greater life satisfaction and meaning. If overwhelmingly negative and inhibiting emotions are part of your life, your life reflects a lesser experience. This is the undisputable and inarguable math of life quality. Your responsibility and challenge is to manage and leverage the forces and activities within your life in ways that nourish your sense of well-being, and ultimately, your life. In short, a quality life is about designing a life around the activities that empower you and your quality of life.

Life Modeling

As I began to appreciate the profound role that activity plays within life and living, I also became intensely aware of and curious about the potential for "engineering" specific qualities into life, or "*Life Quality Modeling.*"

Admittedly, the idea of designing life beyond choosing a religion, your degree, employer, or life partner is rather compelling stuff. One day I was speaking with a colleague about life modeling. We both wondered if it could be taken too far. Instantly, thoughts of little girls with poufy hair in beauty pageants and children playing sports they had absolutely no interest in came to mind. Practically speaking, "over-modeling" is something few would or could tolerate in their own lives, and is not something of particularly great concern. Modeling your own life is very different than someone else modeling it for you.

The idea behind life modeling is rooted deeply in pursuing specific activities that reinforce and support the quality of life you seek, and minimizing those things that detract from it. We all model our life to one degree or another. Consciously designing and building your life around your particular passions and interests offers considerable appeal and advantages to most people. However, it's often something we put on the back burner as a task that we'll "get to someday."

While life modeling offers compelling advantages, it also has requirements. The first step to achieving a higher quality of life is to take the responsibility of your life and its outcomes. This is only possible by taking responsibility for your life. This simple concept provides a profound standard to guide you through your life's journey.

So, is that all there is to living a high quality life? Well, not exactly. A high quality life has ongoing nutritional requirements and emotional needs. If you don't provide what it needs to thrive, the quality life you've always dreamed of will disappear as quickly as it came into view. That's why we call it *living* a high quality life, not having, possessing, or owning a high quality life. As it turns out, a high quality life has quite a voracious appetite for affirmation. Unless you're committed to living a quality lifestyle, you'll never experience it – or at least not for long.

We'll explore more of these concepts in the third section of this book. For now, let's discover what kind of things can screw up the whole mess!

FLIES IN THE OINTMENT

A quality life is truly an amazing thing. Like everything else in life, it comes with its own set of built-in distractions - a few of which wreak havoc on those wanting to pursue a more satisfying and rewarding life.

Life is full of qualities – bazillions of them, in fact. Yet, no single quality is perceived the same between two individuals. One person may find a theatrical performance to be enlightening and enjoyable. Another might find that same experience boring and trite. When it comes to life's qualities, beauty truly is in the eye of the beholder; and mixing beholders can be the recipe for a wonderful day at the beach - or the perfect storm!

The importance individuals place on the qualities within their lives also varies considerably. One person may place a profound emphasis on intimacy while another tries to avoid it altogether. Each of us attaches unique significance to the qualities within our lives based on our experiences, beliefs, fears, and personalities. Regardless of the reason for our perceptions, or the qualities within our life, we always justify our life's design. Our reasoning becomes the foundation of the life we design and experience.

When we intermingle with others, our life qualities and values take on new and more interesting roles. When two people with similar or complimentary life values form a relationship, they will most likely get along well and their value will combine to create something far greater than the sum of their parts. Individuals with dissimilar life values, on the other hand, often work against each other's efforts, and frequently undermine or inhibit their collaborative potential.

However, be careful before judging a book or individual by his or her cover. Before you start searching for that perfect life or business partner based on similarities between them and you, understand the distinctions between life qualities and the outward manifestations of personal behavior. They are not the same. In many cases, relationships between two apparently opposite individuals thrive. This is because, despite having different behaviors, the life values both share are similar or complimentary. First impressions are rarely accurate when it comes to revealing life qualities.

The second fly in the ointment is a bit more challenging. Many people assume they can simply "create" a quality life. It doesn't quite work that way. If it were that easy, everyone would be living the good life and I would be writing books about photographing lorikeets in Australia!

A quality life simply is or isn't. There are no "part-time," "in-between," or "sometimes," in the world of quality lives. Unlike the life we all possess by default, a "quality" life requires specific conditions to be present before it can exist. Think of it as a musical play. Before the play can take place, actors, singers, the orchestra and everyone behind the scenes must be present and in place. Even if a few are absent or out of place, the experience degrades significantly. The same is true about a quality life. However, once the conditions are in place, the experience can be extraordinary!

Your life is a reflection of everything about you and your world. If you desire a higher quality of life, *then live a higher quality life.* Reimagining your life around activities and functions that are most important to you, return the greatest emotional benefits, and allow your life and sense of wellbeing to grow and thrive.

The quality of your life defines your sense of well-being and contributes energizing and liberating results including self-confidence, empowerment, enthusiasm, resilience, overall satisfaction, and happiness. The results of a quality life benefit you in a myriad of ways that range from happier and healthier living to simply feeling great about every day. It's another of life's remarkable chemistry lessons that adds dimension, intrigue, and depth to humanity.

Where It Fits

Your sense of well-being and life quality is defined by how you feel about yourself and the life you live. If your sense of well-being contains highly positive aspects, you respond with a greater sense of satisfaction and pleasure – all the stuff of a high quality life. If these qualities are not expressed, you experience a considerably lower quality life.

The overarching idea behind a more meaningful and satisfying life is to reinforce your sense of well-being with positive and nourishing qualities from a passion-driven life.

Practical Life Design Strategy

When thinking about what you have just read, and your life, please explore the following questions.

8.1 What is a life quality?

8.2 How are life qualities formed?

8.3 Why are life qualities formed?

8.4 How can living get in the way of experiencing a high quality life?

8.5 What are some common reasons people fail to experience a high quality life?

8.6 What does it mean when it is said that things like money and fame most often inhibit a life of quality?

8.7 If you have money and fame, does this mean that a high quality life is necessarily impossible? Explain why or why not.

8.8 What is it that a "high-quality" life provides you?

8.9 How are life qualities created?

8.10 Can you influence the quality of your life? If so, how?

8.11 What is a low quality life?

8.12 How do low quality lives come to exist?

8.13 Why is it said that a high quality life cannot be created, it can only exist?

8.14 Why does a high quality life require constant reinforcement?

8.15 Is it possible to live a high quality life part-time – and why?

8.16 What does the term "life modeling" mean?

8.17 If a high quality life is a reflection of how you live your life, what does your sense of well-being reflect?

8.18 If a high quality life requires constant reinforcement, how is this practical?

8.19 What qualities are not present in your ideal life?

8.20 What qualities in your life today are the greatest inhibitors to a more meaningful and satisfying life?

8.21 Thinking of your ideal life, which qualities would be present – including ones you do not feel you currently have?

8.22 Thinking of question 8.21, what appealing activities could you include in your life to add these qualities?

8.23 If you were to reimagine your life in its entirety, thinking about the qualities you listed in question 8.21, reorganize your activities with the most important ones at the top.

8.24 When thinking about question 8.23, how would you design the activities in your life to reinforce those qualities in your life?

8.25 To what do you contribute the friendship with your best friend?

8.26 To what do you contribute your disdain of those you find unsavory?

8.27 Thinking of question 8.25, what life qualities do you share, and how do those reinforce your relationship?

8.28 Thinking of question 8.26, what life qualities do you share or not share, and how do those reinforce your feeling about your relationship?

SECTION TWO - LIFE STRATEGIES

One of the most common questions I'm asked is how a high quality life simply "happens." That's not an easy question to answer in only a few paragraphs. However, what we do know is that when specific qualities are present, a quality life can exist and flourish.

In this section, we'll explore the life strategies that virtually all High Q people I have known share amongst each other. These strategies provide substantial benefits and the foundations for the environments that high quality lives require to exist and thrive.

Welcome to Life Strategies.

108 | **Reimagined**

CHAPTER NINE
THE QUALITY LIFE

> *"Like a home, your life is something that requires a solid foundation of reality, security, and practicality along with a splash of whimsy and fantasy."*
>
> ~ Ian Breck

In *Section One*, we learned that our core strategy provides us with the basic functionality model we use to live our lives. However, our core strategy certainly isn't the only strategy we rely on. We rely on strategies to help us understand and address a multitude of life's more detailed aspects more efficiently. We use strategies that provide basic rules and direction for things like relationships, love, our career, interactions with others, education, religion, friends, and more. These are known as *life strategies*.

Life strategies are special for a number of reasons. First, we have lots and lots of them – in fact, thousands! We develop a different strategy for *each* area of our life that requires interaction. Think of your life strategies as templates, or starting points for life and living. However, the most intriguing feature of life strategies can be found in an unusual subset of them that is shared among virtually all people who live high quality lives. These are known as *"ordinal life strategies,"* or more simply, *ordinals*.

The ordinal strategies of High Q people are the same life strategies you use in your own life, albeit with a few important differences. Those who live extraordinary lives tend to define ordinal strategies in far greater detail than do most others. They also weave their ordinal strategies into the fabric of their lives as opposed to keeping them stashed neatly away until they're needed, as do most. As it turns out, it's the comingling of ordinals that appears to be responsible for a great deal of the primordial soup that high quality lives require to exist and thrive. High Q people don't simply use life strategies - they *live* them.

You would think ordinal strategies are things we inherit in the genetic set of Tinker-Toys provided by our parents. Although this makes perfect sense, it's not how it works. Ordinal strategies are developed, not inherited. The High Q people I have researched frequently cite seminal events and others who have influenced their thinking as the primary drivers behind the way they see their lives and the world.

Perhaps the most important story here is the one within. A quality life is designed and experienced as opposed to inherited or purchased. This means you too can experience a high quality life – providing you understand how it works.

So, what do High Q people have to teach us? Lots!

High Q people characteristically tend to:
- be more active
- be happier with themselves
- live lives that are generally more satisfying
- be generally more successful in their endeavors
- possess a strong work/life balance
- pursue their passions and integrate them into their lives
- savor life's more experiential elements
- possess high levels of integrity
- demand more from those they include in their lives
- be less willing to compromise values and ideals
- be socially active and responsible

- rarely retire
- rarely divorce during their high quality life period
- value more refined relationships in their lives
- enjoy enduring, often lifelong relationships
- value learning highly
- apply organic life strategies
- clearly define and understand the specific features of their lives that shape them.

Introducing the "Big 12"

As we've already learned, core strategies provide the general framework we use to live our lives, and life strategies provide the more detailed foundations we need to address specific issues of our lives. An intriguing characteristic of virtually all High Q people is that they share almost all of the following highly developed ordinal life strategies.

Valuing Themselves. High Q people make themselves a priority within their lives and place a strong emphasis on being someone they personally like and respect.

Individualism. High Q people tend to be highly individualistic. They pursue life according to their personal interests, passions, and terms.

Live Life Built Around Passion and Purpose. High Q people are passionate about the design and execution of their lives. They build their lives around what they enjoy, love, and are passionate about.

Valued Relationships. High Q people see the relationships within their lives as extensions of their existence.

Integrity. High Q people demand the utmost integrity from themselves, those around them, and the organizations they support.

Demanding More. High Q people commonly expect and demand higher performance by themselves, the people around them, and the organizations they support.

Independence. High Q people are far more self-sufficient on many levels, but for reasons you might not expect.

Standing for Something. High Q people tend to be active and vocal advocates and examples of their beliefs and passions.

Loving Deeply. High Q people leverage the power of love in everything from the people in their lives to what they do every day.

Lifelong Curiosity and Learning. High Q people are constantly learning and experiencing. Many believe that learning and exercising their natural curiosity keeps them young, healthy, and vibrant.

Active Living. High Q people consider activity to be the currency of a healthy and happy life.

Active Involvement in Their Life's Design. High Q people are actively involved in the design of their own lives.

So, there you have it! Virtually all people who experience deeply satisfying lives share these ordinal life strategies amongst themselves. Individually, these strategies aren't unique. However, when combined with the influences of core strategy, vision, free will, and other factors, these strategies come together to become far greater in power and influence than the sum of their parts.

In the next several chapters, we'll explore ordinals, and the lessons they have to teach us in greater detail.

114 | **Reimagined**

CHAPTER TEN
IT'S SIMPLY A "YOU" THING

"If you don't manage the qualities within your own life, someone else will manage them for you."

~ **Ian Breck**

I hear it constantly from gurus, coaches, and mentors, "you must first love yourself." I'll admit I've always been skeptical of anyone who loves themselves, or tells me to love myself. Admittedly, I'm not entirely sure how such a thing is even possible beyond what self-gratification or narcissism offers. For starters, I really don't think such a thing is possible or remotely healthy. Love is something you give to and receive from others. Loving yourself is quite different than loving others. It almost seems as if we're toying with nature. However, liking and caring about yourself, becoming someone you really like and admire, and making yourself a priority in your own life are quite different and noble pursuits. In fact, they're essential elements of living well.

One of the first characteristics I discovered about High Q people was that, despite having the same personal foibles as everyone else, they generally like themselves and are mostly at peace with who they are. This strategy makes perfect sense once you understand how it contributes to a quality life.

It was at a research conference in Palo Alto several years ago. Several colleagues and I were talking about relationships and I made the comment that I had no desire to become anyone other than myself for anyone; however, I valued the concept of being the kind of person that others want to be associated *with*. Becoming someone different than who you really are indicates a lack of self-confidence and deception. However, being "someone others want to be associated *with*," is rooted deeply in liking and respecting yourself. It's also about possessing those life qualities that you value most within yourself and others.

Unfortunately, valuing ourselves is a concept most people have some problem grasping. Aside from cultural mores, many find it difficult, or at least challenging, to make themselves a priority within their own lives for any number of reasons. In all too many cases, we place ourselves last on our list of life's priorities. This behavior becomes self-destructive when we ignore our own well-being in the interest of satisfying that of others. As it turns out, we're a bit more protective of our physical safety than our own emotional welfare. For some reason, we just don't treat ourselves very well in this area.

So, why do we have so many problems making ourselves a priority in our own lives? Common reasons include social or religious values, and even things like misplaced guilt. We're taught to base our lives around cultural myths that tell us we should be accommodating to, and serve others. This is especially prevalent in many societies with respect to women's social roles. The idea of liking or caring about yourself and making yourself a priority in your own life often appears at odds with the much-venerated concept of service to others we're indoctrinated with. However, placing yourself at the bottom of life's "most important list" is inconsistent with high quality living or personal happiness. If you want or enjoy serving others, make that an activity within your life – but do so as a function of caring for yourself.

Another significant problem is ignorance. The decision to make yourself a priority in your own life is not one of self-centeredness or selfishness. I asked a close friend about what changed her way of thinking with regard to significant changes she had made in her own life. She admitted to "playing the subservient game," and being rewarded with a "cheating husband, two confused kids, and food stamps." Her decision to take back the direction and control of her own life wasn't one of selfishness; it was one of necessity and survival. Today she confesses it was the smartest decision she's made in terms of life quality, value to herself, and to those who depend on her so greatly. High Q people tend to be self-centric in nature. (This is not to be confused with being self-centered - which is associated with arrogance and selfishness.)

THE VALUE OF YOU

So, do you like yourself - *really*? Do you value yourself as a person? It's interesting to note that most people are rather ambiguous when it comes to revealing their feelings about themselves. Rarely will you ever hear someone say, "I like myself as a person," and really mean it.

In real life, "liking you" represents a bit of a psychological leap for many. Self-confidence and self-esteem issues often prevent people from liking or valuing themselves to any meaningful degree. Others associate liking themselves with narcissism, arrogance, or self-centeredness. Still, others simply don't like themselves in any light. Why is it apparently so difficult for people to like themselves? This is something we simply don't understand well.

Despite all of the reasons we find not to like ourselves, even the most determined self-not-likers among us often find it easier to like themselves once others like them first. Perhaps now you can see the interesting link that develops between being a person you like yourself, and one who is liked by others. Valuing yourself can indeed be a confusing and sticky business.

In a high quality life, valuing yourself provides a powerful and essential self-protective mechanism that makes perfect sense. Making you a priority in your own life starts with caring about and for yourself. Although this appears to be common sense, it's a concept few people embrace for reasons I can only speculate. However, once you discover what's involved, I believe self-priority will become far easier and non-negotiable feature of your life.

Valuing Yourself in the High Quality Life

Valuing yourself is an essential element of every high quality life. The great news is that valuing yourself encapsulates four simple activities: 1.) Understanding the life qualities you *want* in your life, 2.) Understanding the life qualities you want *disassociated from your life*, 3.) *Making yourself a priority* within your life, and 4.) Becoming the *person you really like*.

The process begins with exploring the life qualities you want, or envision having as a part of your own life. Whether it's contentment, love, excitement, relaxation, or any other quality of life, you've probably already thought of several ideas. You may also discover even more by exploring the life qualities of those you respect. Explore each quality within the context of your own life, investigate them and explore how you can integrate those qualities into your life through activities, behavioral adjustment, or lifestyle refinement.

Your next step is determining those qualities already present, or at risk for being present in your life that have no place in it. These can include damaging qualities like frustration, jealousy, anger, anxiety, abuse, or other inhibiting influences. These qualities are called inhibitors because they obstruct your life and its quality. Ridding yourself of an inhibitor is sometimes more difficult than noting its existence. However, realizing inhibitors exist and understanding their causes and sources are important first steps toward eliminating their influence. For now, it's good enough to be aware of the inhibitors in your life and their causes. You will address them later, or perhaps they will become unimportant with improved life design.

When it comes to inhibitors in your life, people are often confused about how best to address them. From a therapeutic and coaching perspective, most counselors I've encountered believe dealing with inhibitors head-on is the best track forward. In some cases, that may be the preferable route. However, I've seen more cases where this approach creates more problems than it solves. When exploring your life, make note of your inhibitors, but don't worry about them quite yet - and certainly don't do anything to eliminate them until you know more about what you really want - and what the costs may be. In many cases, I've discovered once someone creates and implements a realistic life design, many inhibitors no longer have what they require to survive, and become unimportant and insignificant on their own.

We've already explored a bit about making yourself a priority within your own life. This starts with first respecting and valuing yourself. It's about treating yourself well and introducing what you love into your life. (Yes, this even includes pampering yourself!) Not only does this focus you on what you enjoy, it also provides a well-needed regenerative break from the world.

If you've always talked about learning to golf, this is the perfect time to explore a league, or simply set up weekly lessons. If you're into cooking, explore new ideas and increase your culinary skill repertoire. (Sorry, preparing breakfast, lunch, and dinner for the family doesn't count!) Consider a cooking class or inviting friends over to "play" with recipe ideas on a specific day – and don't forget the wine! Take the initiative to learn something new like flying aerobatic kites, getting your SCUBA certification, or something you've always wanted to do but never took the time to – like curling! (I just had to find a place for curling in my book. I can't help it – it's in several locations!) You may also simply want to chill. Who could argue with a glass of wine or fresh lemonade, a great book, and a hammock? Schedule a siesta during your day to read a book, watch a movie, work in your wood shop, have tea, or whatever it is you love to do. The choice is yours - it's your life! Design "me" time into your life and focus it around your interests and passions. Most importantly, *ritualize* your time. Never break your schedule – it's the first and most important *non-negotiable* in your new life!

Finally, explore and become someone you truly like and enjoy being around. Think about this one carefully. Think about those qualities you value most in yourself and others you respect and admire. Explore how you might introduce those qualities into your life. What do you really like about you? Where can you use some fine-tuning? By conducting a quick personal assessment and perhaps moving life's furniture around a bit, you'll discover that you're really quite a valuable person despite a few rough edges here and there. Most importantly, discover, visualize, and treat yourself as someone of value, and someone who is valuable to others. Become the person you value, like, and trust. Discover the true you.

Let's face it - valuing yourself can be a challenge, at least until you understand more about it and what it brings to your life. It's also a necessary part of experiencing the high quality you deserve. Take time and understand the influences that make your life uniquely yours, and who you are as an individual. Understand what detracts from you and the quality of your life, and reimagine yourself as someone you truly value – then make it happen! Design and create the wonderful and respected person you truly are. Become someone those in your life respect and embrace. Discover and bring to life the true amazement within you that has been waiting to be experienced!

IN A NUTSHELL

Valuing yourself is an essential element of a high quality life – and it's wonderfully liberating! It's a healthy life choice with remarkable benefits. Valuing yourself and making you a priority within your own life is also an invaluable protective behavior. It's an essential part of becoming the gatekeeper in your life with regard to the people, places, and things you make a part of your life. It's also about doing those things that keep you vibrant and at your best, and becoming someone who is truly valuable and respected.

INSPIRATION

As the owner of your life, taking care of yourself both physically and emotionally are non-negotiables. All too often, we become the last items on our list of what's important and who to care for in our lives. A high quality life is something that is lived and experienced *every day.* It's all meaningless if we don't treat ourselves as individuals that deserve the best life has to offer – and to protect ourselves from what takes us away from our vision of ourselves and what defines our happiness.

PRACTICAL LIFE DESIGN STRATEGY

When thinking about what you have just read, and your life, please explore the following questions.

> 10.1 Why is valuing yourself and making yourself a priority so important?
>
> 10.2 List the top six priorities in your life in order of importance and explain why the order is how it is.
>
> 10.3 When thinking about your "why" answers to question 10.2, reorder your priorities in order of importance. Did the order change – and, if so, why?
>
> 10.4 If you are not already, what keeps you from making yourself a high priority in your life – and why?

10.5 What are the three elements of valuing yourself, and why is each important?

10.6 How well do you make yourself a priority in your own life?

10.7 What is the purpose of making yourself a priority in your own life?

10.8 Explore and perform each element of the four components of making you a priority.

10.9 Identify ten (10) qualities about you that make you amazing.

10.10 Identify ten (10) qualities about you that you could do without.

10.11 When thinking about question 10.9, how are those qualities expressed in your life today?

10.12 When thinking about question 10.10, how are those qualities expressed in your life today – and how can you rid your life of them and their influences?

10.13 Create your "me" time. When is it? What will you do? Why will you do it?

10.14 If you were to design a strategy to make yourself a priority from this point forward, what would it be?

CHAPTER ELEVEN
UNIQUELY YOU

"Society has become a sea of sameness as most people walk away from their individualism to survive. This transforms life into mere existence."

~ Ian Breck

Every High Q person I've ever known is uniquely and unapologetically individualistic. Despite the homogenized masses, High Q people nurture and revel in their uniqueness so much so that they wrap their lives around it and wear it like a flag. Not only does individualism make High Q people more interesting, it may also protect them from the disruptive influences that have become the uninvited realities in the lives of so many today.

So, what's this thing we call *individualism?* In terms of a quality life, an individualist is someone who thinks independently and functions in ways that emphasize satisfying their personal interests as opposed to the collectivistic interests and expectations of other individuals, groups, culture, or society. More simply put, individualists march to the beat of their own drum.

Being an individualist doesn't mean you're selfish or self-centered. Nor is individualism about spiked green hair, black lips, pierced nipples, social awkwardness, or being out of touch with the world. Individualism is about being shamelessly and wonderfully *you* – whatever or whoever that might be.

Individualists earn another important distinction - they make up the vast majority of those who make momentous differences in the world. In fact, individualism is overwhelmingly the most dominant life strategy among every exceptional person I've ever encountered. While individualism is something widely aspired to by many, it's not always welcomed or embraced by society.

Individualism tends to flourish at times when people feel alienated, oppressed, or challenged by injustice and inequity. The 1960's witnessed a massive individualistic wave: the *Youth Movement*. You might know these people better as "hippies." The term "hippie," or "hipster," meant "we are hip (aware) as to what is going on in the world." Expanded awareness was the overriding objective of the youth movement – and it succeeded brilliantly by all accounts.

In addition to increasing social awareness, the youth movement significantly influenced areas like fashion, green living, social consciousness, world politics, and, of course, music. What's more, these folks never split the scene. They are as influential today as ever, but with grayer hair, and names like baby-boomers, grandparents, and senior citizens. Their powerful sphere of influence remains as potent as ever. With active lifestyles, financial resources, and an unassailable capacity to influence society, politics, culture, and government, Hippies aren't ready to hand in their tie-dyed shirts quite yet - and they're still as cool as ever!

Despite being a highly venerated life strategy by High Q people, individualism is not without its detractors or challenges. Hippies discovered quickly that individualism was not particularly welcomed by a society philosophically, functionally, and politically rooted in consumerism and mass predictability. Many feared hippies and their cultural influence and wanted them gone - not the least of which included people like Lyndon Johnson, Richard Nixon, and America's most powerful thug in that day - J. Edgar Hoover.

Even today, in many societies individualism is considered a threat both to establishment and social order. The Japanese are examples of a group-oriented culture. The Japanese tend to rely on group consensus as opposed to individualism. Europeans tend to be culturally socialistic in nature - more oriented toward acting in the best interests of overall society, but not necessarily through consensus. As American's, we like to think of ourselves as highly individualistic, however, we realistically fall on the socialistic end of the scale. We are far more closely aligned with Europeans from a cultural perspective than the idealized individuality so strongly envisioned by our founding fathers such as Thomas Jefferson, who designed America's form of democracy around intrinsically individualistic values.

From a social perspective, societies prefer collectivist behaviors to achieve predictability and social order. Individualism isn't necessarily welcomed, although there is certainly no reason the two can't coexist. In über-traditional Japan, society is rooted deeply in time-honored groups like *Ie* (family), *mura* (village) and *kaisha* (corporation). As participants in these groups, individuals are expected to conform and demonstrate *wa* (harmony) within the group to keep everything moving along nicely and predictably. It's also believed the nail that is sticking up is the one that will eventually be whacked! Anything that disrupts or challenges the harmony (wa) of the group is considered unacceptable. Therefore, it's culturally essential not to be seen as challenging the harmony of the group, or be the nail that's sticking up. In Japan, individualism is inhibited quite effectively by cultural mores. In many other cultures, individualism is suppressed more openly and violently.

As it turns out, discouraging individualism isn't that difficult – at least until the natives become enlightened and restless with their own lives. In many Middle and Far-Eastern and third world countries, brutal dictatorships suppress individualism openly and violently and have done so successfully for thousands of years. In many of these countries, individualists simply disappear never to be heard from again.

Despite the challenges that often confront individualists, individualism is alive and well throughout the world today, thanks largely to rising challenges to personal liberty and corruption that is increasing the distance between the "haves" and "have not's". Individualism is an important, powerful, and liberating characteristic we all possess to one degree or another. However, High Q people openly and enthusiastically embrace individualism in all of its forms and make it a part of their everyday lives and lifestyles.

Where It All Begins

So, is individualism something we're born with, or is it acquired? Individualism is something each of us possesses to one degree or another; it's a powerful ingredient of the human spirit. However, not all individualists begin as individualists, or choose to express their individualistic proclivities as others do. Individualism, at least within the context of a quality life, appears to stem from one of two primary sources: *environmental* or *reactive*.

Environmental individualism is something you're born with – well, sort of. It's actually more of something you're born *into*. If you're born to parents or are raised by persons who possess and communicate a strong sense of individualism, chances are good that you'll develop independent thinking patterns and function more independently based on environmental influences. As with everything else in life, environment matters when you're talking about individualism.

Many high-profile actors, artists, industrialists, and others who have made great differences in society (both good and bad) are products of highly individualistic upbringings. Unfortunately, few of us are fortunate enough to be born with last names that rhyme with "Barrymore," "Kennedy," or "Guthrie!" Luckily, all hope's not lost if you're not related to any of these highly individualistic families.

Reactive individualism is the other flavor. It occurs when an individual makes a conscious decision to take control of their life and its design.

Francesca is a woman I know with two passions – food and family. She has a fascinatingly energetic personality replete with zeal and enthusiasm. She also happens to be an accomplished Italian cook. Her delicious food is always at the center of her life's philosophy of family, friends, and living well. To see her at work leaves no doubt that Francesca is onto something truly delicious!

Francesca's life didn't start out as it is today. Francesca spent most of her life being the person she was "supposed" to be. Her father kept her sheltered from many of life's distractions that all too often took girls away from home. The family business was her life, and she worked in it for over 25 years. She describes her life as one that was designed around serving others. Her own happiness would have to come somewhere down the line – if ever. That's just how it was.

Despite enjoying her job, as well as being the wife and mother of a loving family, Francesca one day found herself at a place where she admitted not being happy, knowing who she was, or what it was she wanted to be. She also had no idea what to do about it. She realized it was time to make herself a priority in her own life and pursue her true passions of cooking, family, and inspiring others – just on her own terms this time.

For Francesca, the realization that she was unhappy triggered her strong desire to focus on what was truly important in her own life instead of living a life focused on the happiness of others.

"For me," Francesca remarked, "my personal dream was to create a space where families of all generations could come together and share the experience of food, sharing, love, and simply being with each other. It's about the love of food, family, and life."

Francesca parlayed her life's desire for fine food and family into a business of her own where she provides a gourmet kitchen and cooking experience in a cucina overlooking a striking Tuscan valley. It's a place where families come together and prepare meals for their own families. She's ecstatic with a life that almost wasn't.

Francesca is a wonderful example of reactive individualism. Once she realized her life was not what she had envisioned, her strong sense of individualism prompted her to take action. Francesca began thinking independently and in new ways that reflected her personal interests and tastes – and modified her life accordingly. Francesca is an increasingly common example of the truly transformative power individualism introduces into the lives of a new generation of persons wanting more from life and living.

Individualism as a life strategy provides clarity and purpose. It is about knowing who you are, what is important in your life and bringing the two together. It's about having the creativity, vision, and determination to design your life around what you love and to serve your personal interests and needs as an individual.

Individualism is very much about independent thinking. Individualists are unapologetic about who they are and what they want out of life. Individualism transforms CPA's into gourmet chefs, nurses into kite manufacturers, office workers into movie stars, and priests into Shakespearian performers! Why not join the others who have made the decision to embrace their individualism and dare to experience their dreams? From a life quality perspective, individualism is the most liberating and transformative life quality anyone can possess.

Your life is yours to design and live. Don't squander your one opportunity to do it right. Dream – then live the amazement of every dream you have! Love your life!

IN A NUTSHELL

Individualism plays an important role within high quality lives because it focuses on independent thinking and emphasizes the importance of your dreams and what places you at your best. Individualism is a wonderfully healthy and immensely liberating life choice that transforms believing in you to an energizing art form!

INSPIRATION

Individualism is a powerful life strategy with so many benefits to offer a quality life. On a personal basis, it frees you from many of the constraints and dictates of society and culture. Individualism enables you to live your life as you desire and on your own terms.

From a High Q perspective, individualism plays roles as both liberator and motivator. While freeing you from social and cultural constraints, individualism allows you to focus on what's important to you and gives you pleasure. It also gives you the opportunity to embrace the dream of your passions within your own life. These powerful characteristics are embraced and exemplified by all High Q individuals I've ever known.

PRACTICAL LIFE DESIGN STRATEGY

We're all individualists to one degree or another. High Q people tend to be more aware and actionable with regard to their uniqueness. Instead of relegating it to the second chapter of life, High Q people allow their individualism to become a powerful catalyst for change within their lives today.

Let's take a moment to explore your personal individualism - and create a picture of who you really are – or could be! Answer the following questions while remembering that an individualist is someone who thinks independently and functions in ways that focus on satisfying their personal interests and ideals as opposed to the collectivistic interests or expectations of any group, culture or society.

11.1 How do you see yourself as being different from other people?

11.2 How do you consider yourself uniquely talented?

11.3 Do you view yourself for who you really are - and are not? Explain.

11.4 Are you honest with yourself about your personal shortcomings? Can you talk about them without embellishing or whitewashing them? Why or why not?

11.5 Do you connect easily with others who are individualists?

11.6 Do you enjoy encouraging others to pursue their dreams, dare people to be different, and support those differences?

11.7 Do you identify with specific social causes?

11.8 Do you enjoy sharing your knowledge and expertise?

11.9 Are you exposed to learning from and interaction with other individualistic people?

11.10 How do you spend your time alone?

11.11 What risks do you take?

11.12 How do you respond to failure?

11.13 Do you encourage individualism and try to instill your individualistic values in your family and friends? Why or why not?

11.14 If you were to design a strategy about embracing your individualism from this point forward, what would it be?

As you can see, saying you're an individualist and being one are two very different things! Most of us are not nearly as individualistic as we would like others or ourselves to believe. Being individualistic ultimately falls back on your capacity to think independently and act on behalf of your personal interests.

High Q people are unique because they understand what makes them who they are, how they're different, and what they want and don't want in their lives. This makes it easier for them to think independently, and enables them to focus their attention and decisions on what is important to them and their happiness.

The true magic of individualism in the High Q life is *you*. Embrace you every single day of your life!

132 | **Reimagined**

CHAPTER TWELVE
A LIFE OF PASSION

"Passion is energy in its most thrilling form. Passion focuses you on the excitement within your world!"

~ **Ian Breck**

I'll admit it - *I'm addicted!* I absolutely love brilliance! I'm passionate about it! I don't care how you slice it, pack it, or present it; brilliance simply turns me on! Jake Shimabukuro playing Queen's *Bohemian Rhapsody* on his ukulele and the awe-inspiring Trans-Siberian Orchestra never cease to amaze me and those whom I introduce to their music. A friend of mine, singer/songwriter Natalie Riccio is one of the most amazing yet undiscovered talents I've ever known. I once had the privilege of seeing Denny Dent literally dumbfound the audience with his "*Two-Fisted Art Attack*" in New York. (He died all too soon in 2004 - ironically from a heart attack. Brian Olsen, Denny's only protégé, carries on Denny's energetic legacy.) Give me the brilliant spectacle of a flash mob any day of the week! Tony Royster Jr. delivered arguably one of the most jaw-dropping drum solos in history – when he was only a 12-year-old kid! He still lights the skins up today. Who will ever forget Susan Boyle's unexpectedly amazing *I Dreamed a Dream* from *Les Miserables* on *Britain's Got Talent*. Exceptional movies like *August Rush, Something's Gotta Give, Bottle Shock,* and *Under the Tuscan Sun* take me places unexpected in the world and within myself. Of all of the things this world has to offer, passion is one thing that makes life worth living - and the world's a much more amazing place to be because of it. Passion is life's volume control.

Passion works *both* ways - it's not just a happy/amazement sort of thing. Passion can also be a disgust/contempt experience as well. I'm passionate about the reprehensible people, companies, and governments who feel empowered to invade and devalue the lives of others for their own gain. I find it disgusting that these few thousand pieces of excrement have all but destroyed the American dream and at the cost of a seriously wounded citizenry left to pay for their greed and avarice with no culpability. Unfortunately, they've never been, and probably never will be, prosecuted.

There's passion at work! Now, can you understand why I call passion life's volume control? The true value of passion is argued openly among experts today. Because of passion's propensity to ebb and flow for little or no apparent reason, some consider it an unstable and volatile emotion of limited value. Others go one-step further and consider it useless altogether! However, when it comes to quality of life, passion is essential to those who embrace it and consider it an essential element of the high quality life.

Passion is one of life's most intriguing, yet misunderstood qualities. In contrast to those who believe passion is useless, virtually all High Q people elevate passion to new heights in terms of both survival and quality of life. Once you understand a bit more about passion, it becomes apparent why.

So, what is passion? Passion is a powerful and heightened emotional state and response to anything. Although some feel passion is of little value, passion releases endorphins, adrenaline, and other chemicals that influence our senses of well-being - both good and bad. From a psychological perspective, too much passion may be a double-edged sword. Scientists are beginning to link extreme passion with depression.

Within the context of a quality life, passion typically comes in one of two flavors: *short-term* and *long-term*. Short-term passion is an initial motivator that sparks your interest in something or someone and compels you to explore it further. Long-term passion provides enduring reinforcement that inspires you to continue your relationship with a particular person or activity. I refer to long-term passion as *inspirational*, and short-term passion as *perspirational*.

Passion in the High Quality Life

Humans thrive on pleasure. High Q people are often passion junkies and have no problem admitting it. They not only seek passion, they weave it into their lives. If the drug of choice for the rest of the world is cocaine, passion is what makes the toes of High Q people curl.

A friend of mine, Mike, stunned his friends, colleagues, and family by walking away from the seven-figure world of Manhattan's elite advertising industry to become a gentleman farmer in Connecticut. Today Mike raises and sells organic vegetables and flowers for locavores. By the way, he's also happier than he ever dreamed possible.

We were at lunch one day, and the topic of life changes came up. As someone who decided that drastic changes were in order for his life after the passing of his father at a relatively young 62 years of age, Mike credited his decision to pursue his passions for returning his life to a far more meaningful state of existence. It was something Mike would have never considered in his previous life, but something that became a transformative force within his life.

"Having lived in the city (New York City) for over 20 years, gardening and the things I really enjoyed weren't much in the cards for me," Mike recounted. "Dad and I worked together in the garden when I was a kid. We always had a great time and were constantly experimenting, learning, and growing cool things. Despite his passing, dad is always with me in my garden today. We still grow really cool stuff."

Mike admits that his new life didn't happen overnight. In fact, he admits questioning his move and wondering openly if he had made a mistake on several occasions. However, once he stopped trying to accomplish everything at once, stopped second-guessing himself, and began tackling life one-step at a time, he realized he'd made the right decision. It was then, he says, he discovered the value and meaning of life's true journey.

"Passion is what life's all about – but I don't think most people realize, know what to do with it, or are comfortable with putting it to work in their own lives," Mike noted. "I find it interesting that each of us has an idea about what we would do if we won the lottery, but seem content to wait until that time comes to pursue what really turns us on in life. With thinking like that, it's no surprise that achieving meaningful happiness is such an elusive goal to most people."

Mike is a perfect example of someone who has discovered the benefits of merging passion and life. Integrating passion with life is an integral pursuit of a high quality life. It often seems as if High Q people are on an endless search for everything from the most decadent cupcake to the most enthralling theatrical performance to feed their addiction and add another chapter to their lives. Who can argue with that?

Integrating those things you are passionate about into your life can be a challenge, but it's also an extraordinarily rewarding and satisfying experience that provides value, contentment, and happiness to your sense of well-being and quality of life.

In the context of a quality life, there are three basic levels of passion integration. When exploring the following passion types, please remember that passion goes both ways – good and bad.

Passive Passion

Benefit: Returns limited emotional and life quality results.

Passive passion requires little, if any significant involvement by you. You might be passionate about sports or news, sit and watch it on television with only a limited emotional or life quality response.

Active Passion

Benefit: Returns substantial emotional and life quality results.

Active passion requires you to be involved in the scene to one degree or another. If you are interested in wine, you actively go to places to explore and pursue your passion on a regular basis. If you are an activist, you do the same. In short, you contribute to your passion through participation.

Integrative Passion

Benefit: Returns substantial and complex emotional and life quality results.

Integrative passion is something you build into your life. For example, if you like to work with wood, you might decide to take woodworking beyond the active passion stage to a level where it becomes a business or stronger commitment than a hobby.

As you can see, the degree to which you integrate passion into your life determines the benefits you receive from it. Balanced and appropriate integration is always the key to overall success.

When talking about life, however, more passion isn't always better. Many who have attempted to turn their passions into a business have destroyed both the pleasure of their passion and their quality of life. Despite having a passion for something, some simply don't have the mindset for business.

While short-term passion is useful to direct us toward things of potential interest, it's not necessarily an indication that the pursuit should be continued. Some become so addicted to the rush of passion, that once it begins to wane, their sense of well-being, and ultimately their commitment, falls like a rock! This can be easily observed in certain relationships. Beware of any relationship (interpersonal or otherwise) that is heavily passion-centric or irrational. Such relationships are often destined for failure as the emotional rush of the passion can break down – which it usually does.

Like everything, passion has its dark side. I know individuals who are little more than serial daters because of their inability to experience continual emotional "rushes" within their relationships. To these people, the effects of passion are quite addictive - and often devastating to those unknowing participants on the other side of the relationship. This is a powerful example of passion's primary weakness - it makes no distinction between right and wrong.

Properly leveraged passion is an important driver in a quality life, providing you understand its limitations and pitfalls. Passion is best served with a healthy serving of rationalization and common sense.

Follow your passion and explore further those things that pique your interests and curiosity. If your passions continue to inspire you, explore them more deeply and allow yourself to become creative with them in your life. Allow your passions to guide you toward new people, places and activities and embrace the opportunities they introduce.

In a Nutshell

As life's volume control, passion is a powerful element within the high quality life. Allow it to guide you to new ideas, and to focus you more closely on those things that intrigue and stimulate you. Embrace passion within your world and allow it to contribute excitement, direction, and meaning to your life.

Always keep in mind the nature of passion. Passion is easily influenced and misguided. Never rely solely on your passion to make any decision. Passion without reason is reckless and dangerous. Always temper your passion with healthy doses of common sense, reason, and pragmatism.

Inspiration

A life devoid of passion is what so many people are running from today. Passion is exciting, sexy, intriguing, and breathes life into our existence and makes us feel young again! As with anything, however, too much of a good thing is usually a bad thing; passion is no exception.

Passion adds zing to life and living. It motivates, inspires, and reinforces those things we both love and loathe. Listen to your passions and follow where they lead you and your life. Build them into you, your life, and the life you share with others.

Practical Life Design Strategy

The first step in living a life filled with passion is to discover your own personal passions. Let's do it!

Please explore the following questions.

12.1 List at least 10 those things you are passionate about – in a positive sense.

12.2 List at least 10 those things you are passionate about – in a negative sense.

12.3 Write down the things you might like to explore further, but haven't done so yet. Also note why you have not followed them to this point.

12.4 Take your life journal with you throughout your day and write down the things you encounter that touch, inspire, amaze, and interest you. As you think of an item or activity, write it down!

12.5 Go back to your *positive passions* that you outlined in question 12.1. Explore each one and how you could experience more of that passion in your life.

12.6 Go back to your *negative passions* that you outlined in question 12.2. Explore each one and how you could lessen the influence of, or become an activist against, each in your life.

12.7 When thinking about question 12.1, identify each passion's type (passive, active, and integrative), and determine if it's properly positioned, how each should be positioned – and why.

12.8 When thinking about question 12.7, and the passion types you list for your activities, what does the cumulative pattern suggest about your personality and/or behaviors?

12.9 When thinking about question 12.1, if you were to design your life around each passion, what would your life look like?

12.10 When thinking about question 12.2, if you were to design your life as an activist around each negative passion, what would your life look like?

12.11 When thinking about your answers to questions 12.9 and 12.10, which lifestyle has the greatest appeal to you and why?

12.12 If you were to design a strategy about living a life around your passions from this point forward, what would it be?

CHAPTER THIRTEEN
RELATIONSHIPS

"The person least involved in the relationship controls it."

~ **Ian Breck**

When I first began exploring High Q people, I was dumbstruck by the relationships they had with almost everything in their world. It wasn't so much the relationships themselves as the way they "*used*" their relationships that struck me most. It was as if they'd built their entire lives around the relationships in their lives that ranged from people to plants. If something was part of their lives, it often had a story behind it.

Unlike most people who accumulate possessions throughout their lives, High Q people tend to gather relationships with a greater sense of purpose. If something doesn't have particular meaning or a story behind it, it's nowhere to be found in their lives. Unlike most who tend to take relationships for granted, High Q people value relationships highly, and also more strategically than others. Whether it's a life partner, a play, a car, a job, a real estate agent or a tailor, relationships in High Q lives are exceptionally valued elements of life's experience.

If *core strategies* provide an overarching life model, and *life strategies* provide granular models for things like how we love, treat ourselves and the like, *relationships* provide the knowledge and instructions we use to interact with our world. While knowledge provides important understandings about anything, relationships describe our connection to those things. You have a relationship with your partner. You also have one with your pet, your refrigerator, your job, and the world surrounding you. Everything you encounter results in a relationship – it's one of the human design's greatest features. From a cognitive perspective, a relationship is the brain's way of packaging what we know into a compact and easily accessed container. As it turns out, it's also a powerful cognitive performance strategy.

The easiest way to understand relationships is to think of them as *connections*. If you love chocolate, you have developed a positive connection (relationship) between yourself and chocolate. (The *verb* you place between you and anything identifies your overall relationship with it. In this case, you obviously have a thing for chocolate!) Your relationship with chocolate is far more than yumminess. It's a conceptual envelope that contains all of the information you associate with chocolate. It includes descriptive characteristics like color, feel, smell, taste, and what to do with it when it gets in your hands. It also returns value to your life. When you see a piece of chocolate, your brain recognizes it based on the characteristics stored within your relationship of it.

We use relationships to make sense of our world. Without them, we would eat clouds; make love to trees, and drive cuckoo clocks. Life would pretty much be a Felliniesque freak show.

So, what makes relationships so different from a quality life perspective? It's not that the relationships themselves are different. They're not. They've simply been promoted to building block status. High Q people have a propensity to seek, refine, and manage their relationships with an eye toward their ideals and requirements. It's not about the bakery; it's about the relationship you have with the people who work there. It's not about the car; it's about your relationship with the company that sells and services it. It's not about the person; it's about the relationship you share with them. It's not about the job; it's what it contributes to your life. If the relationship isn't working out, it's removed from the scene. In the final analysis, high quality lives are built around high quality and highly valued relationships.

Leveraging Relationships

The most important thing to understand about relationships is that each one returns qualities that either contribute or detract from your life. If your relationship with something or someone is reinforcing, it contributes positively to your sense of well-being and quality of life. If not, it becomes an inhibitor or liability and should be addressed appropriately. Although understanding the nature of the relationships in our lives is imperative, many researchers are coming to believe it's *how* we connect to our world that is most important.

How we address relationships and relate to others is believed to have its roots in childhood. One widely accepted theory suggests that we employ one of three possible strategies when relating to others: *secure, anxious* and *avoidant*; all of which are influenced by the relationship we have with our parents and caregivers as children. The *secure* child appears to be confident with their caregiver and feels empowered to explore their world safely. The *anxious* child perceives their caregiver as being unpredictable, and subsequently becomes immersed in acquiring the love of that caregiver. The *avoidant* child sees their caregiver as rejecting them. They tend to discount their own needs. The significance of such behaviors is that, once developed, some artifacts tend to remain throughout life – *but are not necessarily predictors of adult behavior.*

To explain relationships even more concisely, a six-part model was created that sets out to define specific attachment styles we share with others.

ATTACHMENT STYLES

Agape (Pronounced "*AH-gah-pay*") Selfless, spiritual, patient, undemanding, and giving. Examples include parental love, a teacher's interest in his or her students, or a doctor's care for his or her patients. Many consider this style unrealistic in romantic relationships because no return of love is expected.

Eros Passionate, self-assured self-disclosing: enjoys intimacy. Some describe this style of attachment as clingy. It's often short lived, although it can transition into other attachment styles.

Pragma Requires that both the partner and relationship meet certain criteria and objectives. This style may appear to be unemotional and cold. However, once a partner is found, it is believed other styles of love can develop.

Storge (Pronounced "*STOR-gay*") Friendship-like, supportive, and reliable. It usually starts as a friendship that slowly develops into love. If the love ends, it is gradual. However, the friendship usually remains.

Ludus Fun, exciting, prefers multiple partners. It does not require deep emotional involvement. It's is about fun and enjoyment. "Nothing serious" is the motto of ludic relationships.

Mania Dependent, jealous, conflicted: yearns for love but experiences disappointment. This style of relationship is associated with massive highs and cavernous lows like a roller coaster. It's also highly sensitive. One wrong statement or misperceived notion and the cars are off the rails!

CHART 13.1

People possessing one of the first four attachment styles often associate with others of the same style. The last two attachment styles, however, are not quite as discerning. They often intermix with other styles, which may benefit them by providing a stronger partner in the relationship.

From a research perspective, attachment styles have always been of particular interest to me. I've worked with them for years within the context of relationships. However, I also believe these same attachment styles can be applied generically to all relationships – including ones like those we have with companies, objects, and intangibles like religion or theory.

Craig is a friend of mine who accepted a new position with a firm in Connecticut. His new job required that he and his wife move east from California. They decided to build a new home in Connecticut instead of purchasing an existing one, as they planned on staying permanently and starting a family. Being new to Connecticut, they selected a builder based on the recommendation of their real estate agent. After learning more about the builder, he would be best described as having a ludus attachment style that was happy-go-lucky and never shaken. He was not deeply involved with Craig or his wife, but was otherwise a competent builder. Both Craig and his wife's attachment styles, however, were storge, which meant they were more of the communication and detail-oriented types. Throughout the project, Craig and his builder's different attachment styles resulted in frequent conflicts. Craig commented that if he had it all to do over, he would have selected a different builder despite being pleased overall with the quality of his builder's work.

Curious about Craig's thought process, I contacted several friends to explore why they select the companies they do. As it turns out, each person had an ideal attachment style for the type of resource they employed. Almost all preferred real estate agents and doctors of the storge attachment type - friendly and trustworthy. Each desired a mechanic with a pragma attachment style - functional. The reason we migrate to specific people, places, and things is probably more closely associated with our ideal expectations from each relationship we encounter.

Interestingly, you're probably drawn to and remain with companies that align with your attachment style expectations. Companies would be well advised to understand the attachment styles their customers expect, and work to provide that style and keep in line with customer expectations.

Relationships are natural elements of our lives with critical roles to play. However, *how* we relate to our relationships probably plays an even more significant role in how our relationships contribute to the quality of our lives. Leveraging relationships creatively begins with understanding the nature of those relationships, and ultimately your expectations from them.

Understanding the nature of and how we use the relationships in our lives can also help us explain why some relationships fail and others thrive. With this knowledge in hand, you can more actively manage and leverage the relationships within your life.

Once you've developed the ability to understand and leverage your relationships effectively, become creative with them. Begin developing and nourishing relationships that you want to include in your life. Embrace and nourish those relationships provide qualities that increase your sense of wellbeing and life quality. Don't be afraid to edit or even eliminate those relationships that fail to meet your expectations, or no longer contribute positively to your life. Only then will you begin to experience the true amazement healthy relationships provide both our life and living.

In a Nutshell

Attachment styles are powerful concepts that go far in helping you understand the dynamics of the relationships in your life. Know them. Use them. Make them a part of your daily vernacular.

Be mindful of and creative with attachment styles and your relationships. By matching a particular attachment style with your expectations of a relationship, you will discover relationships that are likely more rewarding by their very nature. Align your relationships with your expectations, and ultimately increase your quality of life in the process.

Practical Life Design Strategy 1

Let's take a closer look at the attachment styles in your life.

13.1 Thinking about yourself, would you describe your upbringing as secure, anxious, or avoidant? Why do you say this, and what has it meant to your lifestyle.

13.2 Thinking about yourself, what attachment style best describes you? (Use CHART 13.1)

13.3 Thinking of your existing partner, how would you describe their style of attachment? (If you have no current partner, skip this question.) (Use CHART 13.1)

13.4 Thinking of your ideal partner, how would you describe their attachment style? (Use CHART 13.1)

13.5 Thinking of your current partner and your ideal partner in terms of style attachment, how does your existing partner compare to your ideal partner? (Use CHART 13.1)

13.6 List at least five (5) companies you use along with their attachment style as perceived by you.

13.7 When thinking of the types of companies you listed (beauty salon, mechanic, etc.), what attachment type would you consider to be ideal for each type of company? (Use CHART 13.1)

13.8 When thinking about the companies you listed in question 13.6, how do the companies you support differ from your ideal expectations in question 13.7? (Use CHART 13.1)

Types of Relationships

I began this chapter with the quote, "*The person least involved in the relationship controls it.*" I included this is because I believe it's essential to appreciate the value and impact relationships introduce to your life, and what they contribute to your life's quality. Whether it's a friend, an activity, or anything else, when you engage in a relationship, you create pathways into your life that introduce influences with the potential to alter it profoundly. This is precisely why great care is required of the relationships you allow within your life. The nature of the relationships not only determines what they bring to your life, but also who or what controls and defines your life.

Not all relationships are created, or at least end up being equal. We can break relationships into three distinct sub-types.

Isometric relationships are relationships where each party values the other *equally*. Within the context of intrapersonal relationships, this assures optimal interaction and mutual reward. For other relationships like those you may have with a market or product, the reward you receive from the relationship is equal to or greater than the cost of your interaction. Isometric relationships are beneficial to your quality of life provided the interaction is positive and affirming. When the interaction is negative, confrontational, or abusive, such relationships should be altered to the positive when possible; or otherwise avoided if positive change is unattainable.

Superior relationships are those where *one party of the relationship values you more than you value them.* In intrapersonal relationships, this can cause serious problems; but may be advantageous in some business situations. For relationships like the ones you have with a car dealer or health expert, the reward you receive from that relationship is often far greater than the cost of your interaction. Superior relationships can provide important elements to a quality lifestyle providing the interaction is beneficial and non-abusive.

Inferior relationships are those where *you value others more than they value you.* Inferior relationships are rarely beneficial and have no place in a quality life. With regard to intrapersonal relationships, the results can be catastrophic. When it comes to other relationships, like the ones you have with a business or your career, the rewards are often far less and the costs of your interaction are often expensive in terms of commitment and ultimately satisfaction. In most cases, inferior relationships are detrimental to a quality life and *should be avoided.*

Managing Your Relationship Portfolio

Throughout life, you accumulate a collection of relationships in what I call your *"relationship portfolio."* These relationships are powerfully influential elements of your life because of what they contribute to your life's quality. Because you rely on them so intensely and their influence is so deeply influential, the relationships of your life must be managed with great care.

I was talking with a client about relationships and he mentioned how much more important relationships had become in his life over the years. Of all of the positive things that relationships provide, we both acknowledged they also could have dark sides. Not all relationships are created equal. Some are enlightening. Others are far less so. The challenge is to evaluate relationships honestly and edit the relationships in your life to ensure the optimal health of your relationship portfolio and quality of your life.

Relationships are not automatic, auto-renewing, or self-healing. They require nourishment, respect, patience, and constant care. Relationships have a natural course and can change over time, as do you. When any element of a relationship is compromised, the overall relationship suffers accordingly.

In my personal quest for a higher quality life, I decided it was time to evaluate the relationships in my own life. A few inferior relationships had become problematic and were consuming considerable amounts of my time and energy. They were inhibiting the quality of my life.

My personal dilemma with editing relationships is that I firmly believe we're only as good as the way we treat the weakest among us. Two of my relationships, however, were pushing the limits of my empathy. My initial hope was to revive them as positive elements of my life.

The first relationship was one of almost 15 years. My friend and I spoke often - almost daily, in fact. Through the years, his fortunes turned for the worse and he became more negative and condescending about everything in his world. His wife ultimately left him, and he was eventually diagnosed with cancer. Knowing that he needed a friend more than ever, I maintained an open phone line and time in my day to speak with him. Within a year, he began displaying erratic behaviors such as falling off the map for months at a time without telling friends, neighbors, or family where he was or what was happening in his life. These are important things when someone has cancer. On several occasions, the police were called to his home to ensure he was okay.

I, along with many others, made every effort to be there for this person through his challenging times. His outlook simply became more negative and challenging as time went on. On many occasions, I mentioned his aggressive and contrarian behavior and admonished him that such behavior was unacceptable from anyone I would consider a "friend." He assured me that he understood, apologized, and told me it would not happen again. Things would get better for a while, but always returned to the previous damaging behaviors. I finally had enough. Because of my previous warnings, I viewed the final episode as disrespecting my friendship. I decided to walk away from the relationship. As badly as I felt, the nature of the relationship was no longer acceptable and was adversely affecting my own quality of life.

The other relationship was with a family member whose life was spiraling out of control as the result of a lifetime of poor decisions and reckless behaviors. He began treating his family poorly, engaging in numerous affairs and emotionally abusing his family. At the behest of several family members, I was asked to intervene because of the close relationship we shared. I preferred not to become involved, however, at the insistence of one family member and after discovering physical abuse might be involved, I confronted him.

Many of his behaviors were ones I considered dangerous and would never tolerate from anyone. However, I believed an open dialogue would be more beneficial than direct confrontation. Unfortunately, it made no difference.

I sat down one day and asked myself if I would accept this behavior from a friend or acquaintance. The answer was, "*no*." I then asked myself why I was differentiating this person from anyone else in my world. Had this been anyone else, I would have turned my back at the very moment I learned of such behavior. The only differentiator was this person was the fact that it was a *relative*. After a great deal of consideration, I reluctantly told him I no longer wished to be associated with him - and that if I learned of any abuse, every cop in the state would be at his front door in minutes. I reluctantly walked away and left him to his karma. It was one of the most difficult things I've ever done in my life.

I'm not sure I handled either of these situations flawlessly. It was such a difficult and complex thing to do. In retrospect, I doubt there's a perfect solution or way to handle any situation. Often times it becomes a battle between the lesser of two evils. However, my life has value – and I guard it zealously as its *gatekeeper*. When someone doesn't value their life or violates the integrity of their relationships, he, she, or it simply needs to go if they cannot change. As hard as that may be for me personally, the quality of my life and what I allow in it are non-negotiables. The changes I made have resulted in positive differences in my life.

Evaluating and addressing a few problem relationships has taught me several important lessons. First, it elevated the valuable and important relationships that I often took for granted. It also cast a light upon the enormous amount of easily avoidable negative qualities that toxic relationships contribute to life. As far as the "*blood is thicker than water*" argument, it's utter and absolute *stupidity*. If someone doesn't respect a relationship, especially if they're family, the relationship and that individual are flawed. If you allow dangerously flawed relationships in your life, your life will reflect those decisions. Take the responsibility for your life. Walk away from relationships that cannot be made constructive again.

As difficult as it can be, editing your relationships is a necessary and liberating reality of a High Q life. Like many, I used to feel editing relationships was in bad form. However, once I understood the influence relationships introduce into life and life quality, evaluating and editing my relationships became much easier, smarter, and more palatable.

IN A NUTSHELL

Whether it's a relationship with your partner, friend, grocery store, vacation spot, pencil, car, or career, evaluate it honestly and determine the value or cost of that relationship to your life and its quality. Understand your attachment styles, what you expect from your relationships, and what each contributes to your life's quality. If a problem relationship can be reasonably corrected, correct it. Otherwise, don't be afraid to walk away before the relationship becomes toxic. Understand your relationships and what they contribute to your life. Edit them with purpose and clarity.

One of the most revealing insights I've encountered is that how you value yourself often determines the quality of the relationships you are willing to accept in your life. Those who value themselves and their lives highly, tend to protect and define their environment and quality of life with high quality relationships. When individuals value themselves to lesser degrees, they tend to accept lesser quality relationships in their lives. This introduces a multitude of potentially disastrous issues. Understand and value yourself and the relationships you make a part of your life – *then become creative with them!*

The importance of the relationships in our lives is undeniable and obvious. The best relationships not only contribute to our well-being, but also open remarkable windows and doors to amazing new possibilities. Maintaining healthy relationships is an essential part of every high quality life.

INSPIRATION

The influence and complexity that relationships introduce to life quality is beyond enormous. Identify the prominent relationships in your life – both good and bad – and determine what corrections and reorganizations might be in order.

Manage your relationships well. Elevate the important relationships in your life and mitigate or eliminate the ones that offer little or no value.

PRACTICAL LIFE DESIGN STRATEGY 2

Let's take a closer look at the relationships in your life.

13.9 Thinking about your relationship portfolio, which relationships are the most important relationships in your life – and what makes them more valuable than the rest?

13.10 Thinking about your relationship portfolio, which relationships are the least important relationships in your life – and what makes them less valuable than the rest?

13.11 On a scale of 1 to 10, with ten being the highest, how highly do you value you as a person – and why?

13.12 When describing your relationship portfolio, would you say that it expands your world, serves as a crutch or something else?

13.13 If you had an ideal relationship portfolio, what would it look like? What types of people, jobs, and activities would you have in it? What would it provide you in everyday life?

13.14 When comparing and contrasting the answers from 13.13, what would it require to transition your relationship portfolio?

13.15 If you were to design a strategy about how you will address the relationships in your life from this point forward, what would it be?

CHAPTER FOURTEEN
INDEPENDENCE

"We like to think that we are independent. However, when we see all of the things we depend on, we realize how dependent we truly are."

~ **Ian Breck**

One of my greatest passions is blue water sailing. I absolutely love the freedom and exhilaration that comes with being two thousand miles away from the nearest Starbucks. There's nothing quite like waking up to nothing but the whoosh of water on the hull as the wind powers your vessel toward your ultimate destination – wherever that might be. For sailors like me, it's the definitive rush – and the closest we'll ever come to true freedom.

As you might expect, this level of sailing requires a great deal of preparation, experience, knowledge, specialized equipment, and expertise. For even the most experienced and prepared among us, sailing will always be an extremely challenging, albeit exhilarating pursuit. When everything is in place, the journey is spectacular. When anything is lacking, being thousands of miles from nowhere becomes a desperate fight for survival.

More than anything, blue water sailing is about managing dependencies. The more independent you are the better off you'll be. However, that doesn't mean you won't have dependencies, or the dependencies that you have are bad or should be avoided altogether. You'll always require food, water, and health among other things. Ultimately, blue water sailing – and life - isn't a balancing act between independence and dependence, but an exercise in managing expectations and dependencies. The idea of being as independent as possible at sea or on land is flawed. It's really more about being self-sufficient and prepared to deal with life's realities and "what if's" when they occur.

So, what really is independence? When we talk about independence, we tend to think about it in terms of politics or wealth. However, there's much more to it than that.

The dictionary defines independence as…

> 1. Not being influenced or controlled by anyone in your opinion, conduct, etc.; thinking or acting for yourself.
>
> 2. Not subject to anyone's authority or jurisdiction; autonomous; perfectly free.
>
> 3. Not influenced by the thoughts or actions of anyone else.
>
> 4. Not dependent; not depending or contingent upon anything else for your existence, operation, etc.
>
> 5. Not relying on another or others for aid or support.

If you want to understand independence in all of its glory, it's sometimes easier to think of it in terms of *dependence*.

The dictionary defines dependence as:

> 1. The state of being dependent, as for support.
>
>> a. Subordination to someone or something needed or greatly desired.
>>
>> b. Trust; reliance.
>
> 2. The state of being determined, influenced, or controlled by something else.
>
> 3. A compulsive or chronic need; an addiction.

Dependence is the slightly more gregarious sibling of relationships. Relationships contain information about how we connect to our world. Our relationships with things like food and water are obvious – we require them to survive, therefore, our dependence on food and water is high. If the dependence we have on food and water is compromised or unsatisfied, the results are predictable – we die.

In its most basic sense, dependence and independence are measures of our "*need for*" or "*freedom from*" any relationship that exists within our lives. Being dependent isn't bad or good. It can be either. Ultimately, it's about understanding and balancing the relationships that exist within your life, understanding what they contribute to your life and its quality, and ensuring the importance you place on both is healthy and appropriate.

The strength and influence that any specific connection exerts on your life is the measure of your dependence. Dependence describes your "need" for any particular relationship in your life. If you have a high need for a particular relationship like food or water, your dependence is high. If you have little or no need for a snow blower, your dependence is low.

I often hear people remark that independence is preferable to dependence. This statement simply isn't realistic. In most cases, how you manage and leverage a particular dependency is far more important than the dependency itself. A quality life is about balancing dependencies and becoming more self-sufficient where possible. It's also about mitigating the risks of those dependencies you can't avoid.

When you have a dependency for any relationship in your life, you also have a secondary dependency on those things that support that dependency. For example, you might take a medicine that requires a South American plant species for manufacture. If that species becomes extinct, that particular medicine can no longer be manufactured. This creates volatility within your dependency.

As you might expect, needing something and relying on a volatile resource can present serious problems.

Let's look at our dependence on food as an example. We have a *high* primary dependence on food. However, the sources of our food can be quite different. While most of us acquire our food from markets, others grow their own. In this case, our dependence on food is HIGH. However, the *secondary* dependence on the source of our food can be HIGH if we get it from markets where risks to its supply and quality are greater, or LOW if we produce our own and control the quality. In this case, we express our dependence on food as a HIGH-HIGH or HIGH-LOW dependence with the first high or low describing our primary level of dependence, and the second describing the volatility of its source.

The system I use to describe dependencies is derived from a system called a *Williams Dependency Matrix*™. This tool was developed by River Bend Research to describe our dependencies more accurately.

Dependency "Need"	**High-Low** High Need Low Volatility	**High-High** High Need High Volatility
	Low-Low Low Need Low Volatility	**Low-High** Low Need High Volatility
		Source "Volatility"

Williams Dependency Matrix™

The Williams Dependency Matrix (used with permission) describes a "need," or dependence for a particular relationship, and the volatility of the source of that relationship.

Along the left vertical axis you will find the Dependency "*Need*" axis. This axis describes *how much you need a particular relationship*; lower to the bottom and higher toward the top. Along the bottom is the Source "*Volatility*" axis. This describes the *volatility of the source of that relationship*; low volatility to the left and high volatility to the right.

When describing a particular dependency using this matrix, we describe it in terms of something called a "*need/volatility phrase.*" (High-Low, Low-High, High-High, or Low-Low.) The first defines the need, and the second defines the volatility.

Let's explore our dependency for *food*.

Food is a high "need" dependency. This means you'll be working with the top two boxes that start with "HIGH." If you rely on a grocery market for your food, you require a market before you can have access to food. This can be a challenge when a store is not open, closed, bankrupt, or compromised in some way because of loss of power, weather, flood, or anything else. Because of these potential risks, you have a HIGH volatility resource that you rely on to satisfy your relationship with food. Therefore, your dependency on your relationships with food is described as HIGH-HIGH. To ensure your dependency can always be satisfied, having a lower volatility source like a secondary grocer is preferable because it reduces risk and volatility.

To address the volatility and risk, you decide that, if you plant a vegetable garden, have a few chickens and a beef cow, you can reduce the volatility of an external and more volatile resource to satisfy your high dependence for food – and have a healthier source. In this case, your changes decrease the volatility of your relationship with food to LOW. Your dependency for food is then referred to as HIGH-LOW, which is the preferred state for your dependency. This is how dependencies are managed.

Interpreting the Results

Utilizing the Williams Dependency Matrix is a simple three-step process.

First, without regard to your actual dependency need, determine the *ideal* need and volatility for your dependency, and mark the respective quadrants. I often use a star to identify the *ideal* need/volatility quadrant. Remember, this is simply the ideal place where you would like to see your dependency in your life. It's not necessarily where it is right now.

Next, identify the quadrant that best represents your dependency in terms of need/volatility *currently*. I often use a box to identify current need/volatility quadrant.

Finally, look at where you are today with your dependence, and where you ideally want to be. Draw a line from the box to the star with an arrow pointing to the star. This identifies where you need to go to improve your dependency.

Explore several potential ways to reduce either your dependency or your volatility accordingly.

When we talk about our current and ideal dependencies, we refer to each area as *current health* and *ideal health*. When your current and ideal dependencies are the same, they are in balance. Naturally, the idea is to have all of your dependencies in balance.

Let's explore a few examples to get you started.

Dependency: Medication

High blood pressure medication is something that millions of Americans rely on for good health every day. The problem is that each year, thousands of drugs end production for one reason or another, and blood pressure medication often has numerous side effects that can be quite troublesome to patients. The ideal dependency for high blood pressure medications is LOW-LOW. This means that we ideally would have a low need for the medication, but have a low volatility source if the medicine was still required.

As a patient, your current need for blood pressure medication is HIGH. Your resource for medication is also believed to be LOW volatility - but your drug could be dropped from manufacturing, which is becoming a more common occurrence today. In reality, the volatility of your medicine supply is somewhere between low and high. However, you would prefer not to have to take the meds at all, if possible.

Currently: HIGH-LOW (need/volatility)

Ideal: LOW-LOW (need/volatility)

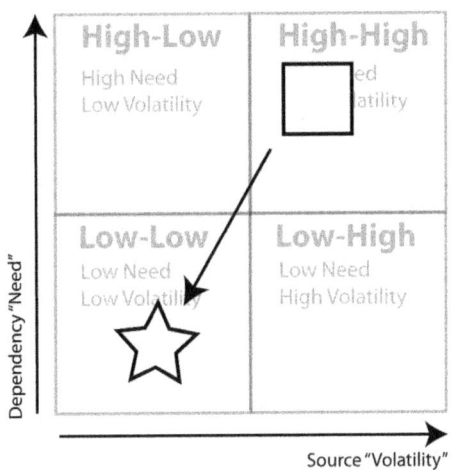

Medicine - Williams Dependency Matrix™

Now that we've defined your ideal dependency levels (LOW-LOW), and your current dependency (HIGH-HIGH), we see that you want to reduce your need from HIGH to LOW based on the illustration above. You don't want to need hypertension medication in the first place. According to your physician, the best way to get off your medication (manage your ideal dependency) is to lose weight, get healthier, eat better, exercise, and do anything possible to reduce your dependency on your medication.

This is the process of evaluating and managing your dependencies.

Dependency: **Your Career**

You've been with your company for several years now. Your job has become merely a job, you have little chance for promotion, and you are not being challenged with your work any longer. Ideally, you would like your job dependency to be less, but also have a stable career where you're more engaged in your job. Your ideal career would be described as having a LOW-LOW dependency.

As your job stands today, it's a HIGH-HIGH dependency because you definitely need your job, but are disengaged from it because you are simply not as interested – ironically, which increases your volatility and places you at greater risk of losing it as well.

In this case, you need to manage your dependency by transitioning to a LOW-LOW career dependency from a HIGH-HIGH dependency.

How would you address this dependency?

Dependency: Relationships

Jane has been married five years. Throughout those years, her husband has lost several jobs. He's also acquired a taste for alcohol and the good life along the way. One evening, the two had an argument over their financial situation. Her husband became angry and almost became physical with her – although she was not physically harmed. Despite that evening, Jane still loves her husband and hopes to get through this rough patch and continue their lives together.

In this example, Jane has a HIGH need for her husband (marriage?), although she clearly has a HIGH volatility partner.

Describe this relationship in terms of its dependency values, and explore a few ideas to realign the dependency and relationship more appropriately, using what you know about relationships and dependencies.

A Real-World Case Study

Kym, worked at a major accounting firm for over 15 years. Her work earned her rock star status and propelled her to an executive partnership in under 6 years, along with a coveted seven-figure salary. One day, Kym simply put down her pen and walked away from it all.

"It's pretty simple, really. I used to think about personal finance and career in terms of providing what I needed to support my lifestyle," Kym admitted. "My salary dictated the car I drove, the house I lived in, and my lifestyle. Like most, I designed my life around my income. Today, I see personal finance very differently – and much more wisely," she says.

Coming from a wealthy family, Kym confesses she never worried about money, or even valued it particularly highly for that matter.

If she wanted something, she purchased it. The money was always there. Her views changed one day when she learned one of her clients had lost virtually everything in the Madoff scandal. "I watched these wonderful people go from supporting charities one day to depending on them the next. One day they came to my office, sat down, looked at me with tear-filled eyes, and informed me that their future had simply vanished. The husband shook my hand, thanked me, and informed me my services were no longer needed. He then put his wife's hand in his, grasped it firmly, winked at her, smiled, and walked through my office door never to be heard from again. I had tears for months. Those two minutes changed my life forever."

That meeting not only changed how Kym perceived finance, but also how she viewed life. "Finance and career had become mechanical to me. My knowledge no longer seemed practical or realistic," she recalled. "Financial independence was about having enough income to afford your life. It was about creating enough wealth to afford the things you wanted and needed. The world is so different today. It has changed - and has given us the opportunity to see how foolish we have been all along. Smart finance is about limiting your exposure to risks so you can survive on less if that becomes your reality – and statistically speaking, it will. It's not a distinction without a difference; the implications are profound. It's a personal paradigm shift that's bad for our contemporary consumerism-based economic model - but the smartest move any consumer can make for themselves and in terms of their quality of life."

In terms of her career, Kym was also seeing the writing on the wall. She had been influenced strongly by the unwelcome financial realities of a changed America, and a life she had yet to realize, but had always contemplated. "The people I worked with were coming in at five in the morning and not leaving until ten at night or later. They told me about their beautiful families, homes, and wonderful lives. I could only imagine them, though - I saw them only behind their desks for what seemed like days on end. They were pale, tired, and had bags under their eyes. One day a partner failed to show up for a meeting. I learned later that his daughter found him hanging in his bedroom closet; eyes half open, face ashen, and body stiff. I shudder at the thought of that being my last memory of anyone – let alone my father. I understood, however, what he must have been feeling before making that fateful decision. He had been pushed so far beyond his capacity that he simply couldn't recover. In this business, we're all replaceable commodities – and we live with that reality. At his funeral, I watched his family uncontrollably sobbing as their father, husband, brother, and friend was lowered into the ground. I realized then how precious and short life really is. I also realized how meaningless mine had become in my own pursuit of 'happiness.'"

Kym spent the rest of the day authoring her letter of resignation. Instead of opting for a detailed colloquy, she kept it simple: "Thank you so much for my career. It's time for me to live now. Respectfully, Kym S."

The next morning she handed her resignation letter to her boss without saying a word. She cleared her desk, offered a few last hugs to bewildered co-workers, and walked through the door never to return. Kym confessed getting into her car and asking herself what she had just done. After about two minutes, however, she smiled and told herself that she had just begun the next chapter of her life. She had just ended her dependence on something that was ultimately destroying her and her life. She's never looked back.

Since that time, Kym has reevaluated her personal career and financial philosophy many times over. "For decades my relationship with finance was always about having more. It was about wealth creation that is associated with greed, risk-taking, and a whole host of other unsavory behaviors I didn't care to have as a part of my life at any level. Things are very different for me today in terms of my relationship with my career and living. Now, it's about minimizing financial exposure, mitigating the risk of an unpredictable world

- and having a glass of wine at sunset! For me, finance has become more about the ability to survive life's "what if's." My relationship and dependency with wealth no longer competes with my relationship with my life. It's very liberating."

Kym had gone through life unaware of the toll her career was taking on her, life and living. Because of a typical seminal event, Kym began rethinking and reimagining her career and life. Once Kym evaluated her career, including the health of her dependence and volatility, she took decisive actions to bring her job and career back into balance. The result was a substantially healthier career balance and a far higher quality of life.

In a Nutshell

The idea that independence is a preferable state and dependence is a less preferable state fails to account for the nuances of the many relationships that are a part of our lives. What makes independence or dependence good or bad has everything to do with the health of the dependencies and what those relationships truly contribute to our lives.

I advise my clients only to worry about those dependencies that are potentially dangerous, like substance abuse, and behaviors that threaten the well-being of themselves or others first. As far as the rest are concerned, it's all about managing, understanding, and maintaining your dependencies in ways that are consistent and supportive of your life quality. Life is about enjoying relationships of all types and flavors. Keeping what is important in perspective through actively managing your relationships and dependencies is a powerful step toward living more beautifully.

Inspiration

Having healthy understandings about the roles relationships play in your life allows you to manage and leverage those relationships more effectively. Understanding your dependencies on those relationships is a critical aspect of the process.

Tools like the Williams Dependency Matrix allow you to visualize the dependencies in your life and the corresponding volatility of those dependencies. Explore and solidify your critical dependencies, and discover ways to seek truly greater independence through self-sufficiency and reduced volatility.

In the end, you'll discover the significant influence that dependencies have on your life and its quality, and how reducing their impact on your life increases life quality significantly.

Practical Life Design Strategy

Let's explore more about independence and dependence in your life.

14.1 When thinking about independence, name 5 things in your life that you would like to be more independent of that would profoundly change your quality of life.

14.2 When thinking about dependence, name 5 things in your life that you would like to be more dependent on that would profoundly change your quality of life.

14.3 When I said that managing your dependencies is more important than eliminating them, what did I mean?

14.4 Why is volatility so important in terms of relationships and dependencies?

14.5 Name 5 examples of dependencies where a HIGH-HIGH dependency is preferable.

14.6 Name 5 examples of dependencies where a HIGH-LOW dependency is preferable.

14.7 Name 5 examples of dependencies where a LOW-HIGH dependency is preferable.

14.8 Name 5 examples of dependencies where a LOW-LOW dependency is preferable.

14.9 When thinking about your list for question 14.1, what are the ideal dependency types for each item on your list?

14.10 Again thinking about your list for question 14.1, what are your current dependency types for each item on your list?

14.11 When thinking about your lists from questions 14.9 and 14.10, what actions can you take to transition your dependencies from the 14.10 to 14.9?

14.12 Repeat questions 14.9-14.11, but use the answer from question 14.2.

14.13 Why is understanding dependencies so critical to a high quality life?

14.14 What role do you think expectation plays in relationships and dependencies?

14.15 If you were to design a strategy about how you will manage your life dependencies and independence from this point forward, what would it be?

CHAPTER FIFTEEN
KEEPING IT REAL

"When anything contributes to integrity, love, beauty, and good within each of us and our world, it is always right."

~ Ian Breck

The single most important principle with virtually every High Q person I've met is *integrity*. From politics, to dealing with the waiter and garbage collector, High Q people openly embrace and value, truth, and integrity. When you look at it more closely, integrity is a powerful strategy that can make wonderful differences in your life.

Integrity is a concept people toss around with reckless abandon these days. It's become cliché and so overused that it causes most people to recoil in a state of skepticism when they hear it.

The dictionary defines integrity as *"adherence to moral and ethical principles; soundness of moral character; honesty."* That's fair enough. However, my personal definition of integrity is "the act of embracing good, repulsing bad, and never allowing the two to intermingle in your mind or life." As it turns out, there's a reason the dictionary and I have such differing opinions – everyone defines integrity differently. As you might expect, that can be a problem.

Integrity is a concept not without its own challenges. First, integrity suffers from having no universal definition, despite that being what makes it so powerful in the first place. I asked several close friends their definition of integrity. None could define it adequately, or accurately explain its function. Try it yourself. Define integrity. What's its purpose?

Despite the fact that none of my friends or colleagues could define integrity particularly well, they openly admit to judging others based on their rather incomplete notion of what it is. Something important enough to influence how we feel about others should be something we also understand well. Unfortunately, that's not always the case.

As if being something that suffers from so many things isn't enough, integrity is also subject to inconsistent interpretation. In other words, one person's morals and ethics aren't necessarily those of another's. If you come from a spiritual background, your conceptual understanding of integrity will likely include religious values. If you were raised in a less parochial environment, your ideas will probably be shaped more around perceptions instilled by your caregivers and environment rather than an omniscient overseer. Because each of us develops distinctive understandings about integrity based on experiences and encounters, integrity is defined and applied differently by each of us. As you might expect, this can lead to problems. When our perception of integrity intersects that of others, a stage for conflict is set. We see the results of such encounters every day in religion, politics, cultures, and governments around the world – and in our own neighborhoods.

Integrity also works in the other ways. I used to joke with colleagues and clients that if a problem could be solved too easily, I personally would step up and redefine that problem! That was humor. Unfortunately, the human animal has become extremely proficient at manipulating and redefining our perceptions of integrity to justify its own interests and pursuits. From selling strategies to political ads and personal politics, complete industries have risen with the sole intention of altering your perception of integrity.

Our perceptions of integrity change as we change. Unlike relationship attachment styles that tend to remain with us throughout our lives, our definition and perceptions of integrity change constantly. This doesn't mean we're flaky. It simply means that our conceptual understandings of integrity are continually evolving, being redefined, and being challenged by life's realities.

THE QUALITY CONTROL NATURE OF INTEGRITY

Whenever you do anything, one of the first things your inner Mozart does is to make a few instantaneous checks for good measure. One of the first is to validate your behavior against your definition and understandings of right and wrong – your integrity. If what you're doing is inconsistent with your perceptions of integrity, Mozart triggers a physical response that gets your attention. Most people describe this as a "rush." Try it yourself. If you were told to pick up an animal and do something mean to it, you will feel uncomfortable about what you were being asked to do. This is your mind warning you that you're about to do something inconsistent with your integrity.

Integrity is also a powerful partner to your decision-making functionality that helps you determine whether your behaviors are appropriate. It's a profound control system and an invaluable survival strategy. Integrity works with us in other ways as well. As a preservation mechanism, we tend to judge the integrity of those around us to determine if they're trustworthy or not. We want to feel safe and comfortable within our environment, and make instantaneous judgments as to our surroundings based on our perceptions of integrity.

When it comes to understanding others, we tend to assess their integrity using one of two strategies: 1.) Perceived *values*, or 2.) Perceived *qualities*.

Some people perceive integrity as more of a value-based proposition. In other words, they associate specific values like honesty, morals, and character with integrity. I refer to this strategy as value-based integrity. People who use value-based integrity tend to apply ideals and values directly to individuals. It's like making a decision to like or dislike someone based on what you believe, or assume them to be, based on their beliefs, appearance, or even linguistic accent or dialect. An example of this might be a gathering where you choose to avoid or engage certain people based on your perceptions (actual or perceived) of the values that person possesses. These values might include something like political or religious affiliations. Despite its many weaknesses and potential for abuse, value-based integrity remains the most common integrity strategy employed by people today.

Other people perceive integrity as more of a quality-based proposition. These people associate integrity with the quality of the interaction or relationship between themselves and others. This is quality-based integrity. Quality-based integrity is based on the quality of interaction or relationship between you and another person, place, or thing. You look beyond what you initially perceive about someone or something, and base your perceptions solely on the quality of your interaction, or ensuing relationship, with that person, place, or thing. An example might be your waiter. If he or she listens to your preferences, then provides exceptional selections based on your tastes and treats you in ways you enjoy being treated, you will most likely perceive her or him as someone possessing greater integrity regardless of how you would have judged him or her by the values of appearance alone.

I once encountered a server punched full of piercings and sporting tattoos all over her body. As the evening progressed, she turned out to be, by far, the best and sweetest waitress I'd ever experienced, despite the fact that I'd expected far less, or at least different service, based on her appearance alone. I absolutely loved the irony and still value the encounter.

Our perceptions of integrity are powerful drivers within both our lives and society overall. We're often too quick to categorize, or separate ourselves from others based on our preconceived notions of specific values like appearance, religious beliefs, political views, or even the self-proclaimed values of others including morality, honesty, and virtue. Throughout my life, I've learned that reality is rarely what it appears to be. Most value-based perceptions actually are artificial constructs with little if any direct correlation or relationship to integrity itself. This is why value-based integrity is of extremely limited value in most High Q lives.

In a Nutshell

Integrity plays a significant role in the quality lifestyle. Developing and knowing your definition of integrity and living the experience offers remarkable rewards that tend to include rather than exclude. For most people, however, understanding integrity more accurately is a significant leap forward in life quality. Once we understand integrity better, we can weave it into our lives with greater constancy, clarity, and purpose.

The integrity strategies we apply in our own lives are not all-or-nothing sorts of things. Although we tend to favor one type of integrity over the other, we commonly intermingle the two depending on the situation. High Q people, however, generally tend to be far more weighted toward quality-based integrity. Most believe this frees them to experience their world while achieving more accurate perspectives through interaction as opposed to the less accurate and more divisive beliefs associated with value-based integrity.

Understanding integrity in your life and how to apply it responsibly to others in your world is an essential element of a high quality life and offers wondrous rewards. High Q people are zealously uncompromising about their personal integrity and that of others they include within their world.

Inspiration

Understanding integrity better allows you to apply it in more dynamic and creative ways, and realize when you may be applying it incorrectly or in inappropriate or limiting ways.

Integrity provides a behavioral throttle and quality control mechanism in quality lives. It regulates our actions and directs us to those things that make us better as individuals, contribute to life quality, and benefit society.

Living a life of integrity completely changes its dynamics. By demanding integrity from those around you, you surround yourself with the quality of people who make life a much nicer place to be. In addition to offering invaluable protections, it frees you to develop safer and more meaningful relationships along your journey.

By demanding integrity from yourself, you make life far simpler and more enjoyable to experience.

Practical Life Design Strategy

Let's define and explore your integrity a bit more closely.

15.1 Define integrity as you see it in your life.

15.2 What is the purpose of integrity and why is that purpose important?

15.3 On a scale of 1 to 10 (10 being the highest or perfect), rate your personal integrity as an individual.

15.4 On a scale of 1 to 10 (10 being the highest or perfect), rate the average score other people would rate your integrity at as an individual.

15.5 What do you believe contributes to your integrity in terms of your behavior, belief, and actions?

15.6 What things would cause you to compromise your integrity?

15.7 Thinking of value-based integrity and quality-based integrity, what are the advantages of each?

15.8 Thinking of value-based integrity and quality-based integrity, what are the disadvantages of each?

15.9 Would you describe your integrity more as value-based or quality-based – and why?

15.10 If you were to design a strategy about how you address integrity in your life from this point forward, what would it be?

Reimagined

CHAPTER SIXTEEN
EXPECTING MORE

"Greater expectations whittle down the possible choices of any decision to a rather blissful few."

~ **Ian Breck**

Have you ever wondered why exceptionalism has given way to mediocrity and indifference? Today, less is what most people have come to expect. We find less all around us in inferior products, poor service, and lowered expectations. We also see it in how people are treated - and how people treat others. We allow unsavory individuals into our world - despite the fact that we would never think of inviting them into our homes. Perhaps the most disturbing fact is that we have come to expect less from everything in our world – including ourselves – and it shows.

It seems as if so many people these days feel empowered to make demands of us - and we often find ourselves powerless to do anything about it. I've always said that those who violate the integrity of our privacy and personal lives should have to live out the rest of their lives under the consequences of what they do to others. Credit card companies raise monthly payments without raising our salaries – without your consent. Banks take money from your account - without your consent. Companies access your private credit and behavioral information – without your consent. Governments raise your taxes – without your consent. The IRS recalculates your taxes and assesses penalties and interest – without your consent. Your phone and communications can now be tapped without your consent or a court order despite the protections the Constitution guarantees its citizens. In a world so "advanced," it appears that everyone's desire to know anything and everything about you and to control you trumps your right to remain private and protected – and there's nothing you can do about it! Or, is there?

You would think that with your life being such an open book and with so many companies and others wanting to profit from knowledge about you, that you would have a voice in the matter. You don't. Expecting to be treated and respected for the profitable repository of knowledge and experience that you are should be a no-brainer. When you have a question or a problem to be resolved, these companies should jump at the opportunity to help you. The great news is that a few do. However, most don't.

Smaller hotels and retail companies dominate the highest positions of virtually all customer satisfaction research studies these days. Banks, cable, and Internet companies are the bottom dwellers in terms of customer satisfaction, and often business practices. The unexpected twist is that while the highest rated companies in terms of customer satisfaction have stock that has performed exceptionally well in recent years, so too have the lowest rated companies. What's wrong with this picture?

So, how do companies with such poor reputations not only survive, but thrive in America today? It's simple: we allow them to. That's right. We expect less. We demand less. We get less. We accept less. We become less. We accept poor service. We accept poor treatment. We accept poor government. We accept inferior products. We accept poor customer service and tolerate others treating us poorly. We tolerate others taking our freedoms and rights without our permission. We tolerate and support companies that move operations offshore to satisfy shareholders while devastating the communities that made them what they are today. We accept companies that tamper with our food supply. We accept genetic modifications to the foods we eat despite having no long-term studies that validate safety – but do have near-term indicators suggesting they may be causing real problems. We accept banks that "legally" take their customer's money from their accounts and illegally foreclose on homes without any civil culpability – all while holding the country hostage with credit and making themselves richer along the way. We tolerate deceptive and fraudulent business practices from financial institutions – but continue to buy their products despite knowing they have been convicted of massively fraudulent activities that have not only damaged their investors, but also decimated an already fragile economy. We accept a government riddled with greed, fraud, incompetence, and pervasive corruption. We accept and make excuses for failure in general. We accept less of everything in our world because that's what we've been left with for accepting less of anything in the first place.

Something's Gotta Give

What we're experiencing today isn't a blip or a fad. Many believe it's the inevitable decline of American society. If nothing else, we're experiencing a profoundly altered social reality from just a decade ago. From a life quality perspective, the changes in our society appear to be fatal. After all, how can anyone enjoy a quality life in a world that has become so innately un-enjoyable?

It's time to introduce some classic German over-engineering to the situation. Allow me to introduce you to Heinz. Heinz is a great friend of mine that I had the pleasure of meeting at a conference in Karlsruhe, Germany. Since we met, Heinz has become a great friend, colleague, and semi-trusted sailing buddy. He, his lovely wife, and wonderfully overachieving children live in the stunningly exquisite canton of St. Gallen, Switzerland.

I had just completed a project that focused on why people "tolerate" - and how toleration affects behaviors and societies. After exploring the premise of my work, Heinz's response was one driven by typical German stoicism. "Don't you think that people generally get what they ask for?" He was right. If we demand less or nothing from those around us, how can we expect anything more, or better to happen? How can we expect change when we don't demand it? As it turns out, tolerance is quite an intriguing concept.

So, have we become a society that demands less and receives exactly what we are asking for – and some say deserve? I believe the answer is undeniably, "yes."

At first glance, the concept of demanding more appears to be a simplistic and rather unremarkable part of a quality life. However, upon closer inspection, it turns out that demanding more is actually one of the more influential and far-reaching strategies that anyone can introduce into their life.

The Power of "No"

It's no secret: Heinz expects a great deal from the people, communities, companies, and governments he makes part of his life. Heinz unapologetically and loudly demands more – and gets it! If people or companies do not meet or exceed his expectations, he doesn't simply walk away; *he shuns them!* Not only will he not patronize them, he also lets others within his personal sphere of influence know exactly why – and they listen. It's not that Heinz is arrogant, aristocratic, snobbish, or a cruel taskmaster. He's actually quite the opposite. He is, however, unremorsefully uncompromising about what he expects from those he makes a part of his life. This makes him the consumer equivalent of a power broker. He demands quality, integrity, and respect. Most importantly, he requires a meaningful relationship.

Heinz is among a growing generation of individuals who are demanding more – and getting it. If you think that everyone Heinz supports has a tough road to hoe, they actually have it pretty well. Heinz simply expects the same level (or perhaps a tad more) of respect and integrity that he offers his own friends and colleagues. Their efforts, however, don't go unrewarded. In return for meeting or exceeding his lofty demands, Heinz becomes the very thing that every person, company, community, or government covets – a powerful and credible advocate.

In the light of a quality life, Heinz's attitude has quite remarkable benefits. Heinz's persnickety nature has resulted in some quite snazzy rewards, as I had the opportunity to experience first-hand.

The day was picture perfect with azure blue skies backed by verdant hills, medieval buildings, and the laid-back vibe of this tiny and otherwise isolated corner of the world. To be quite honest, St. Gallen is almost sensory overload to the uninitiated; it's brain-freeze for the soul. When I'm there, my life becomes a fusion of scintillating bakeries, amazing people, overwhelming markets, restaurants, and scents with no possible explanation or earthly origin as far as I'm concerned. It's different. It's amazing. It's about being alive. It's living.

As it turns out, Heinz has managed to carve out quite the life for himself and his family among the Alps. Despite an already busy life, Heinz somehow manages to be a loving husband, inspirational father, and occasional host to a wayward American looking for a momentary break from his over-the-top life from time to time.

Heinz is an enigma wrapped within Gruyère. Despite being an insufferable professional, he somehow makes the time to drive hours to shop for groceries each week. The stores and he "have this relationship thing," as he puts it. His baker is in the same town, although he occasionally pops into Germany or France to shake up his menu a bit with his wife. She confesses an almost orgasmic addiction to fresh brioche. He buys his produce, beef, and poultry exclusively from local farmers he knows and trusts. He doesn't buy food treated with chemicals or hormones. He once mentioned that we pay closer attention to the television we watch than to what we put in our bodies. On my last visit, we drove to a fish market - four hours south in Genoa, Italy! The trip alone was beyond breathtaking. Heinz makes the trip at least once every other week. I told him his life was ridiculously amazing. He laughed and remarked that it's certainly not overrated, and that everyone should try living sometime!

I've known Heinz for almost 25 years now. He values and celebrates everything in his world. His wife and kids are the center of his life. He loves his 1990-something Mercedes, which still looks and drives like new, his home, and his potentially menacing, although always accommodating once you get to know him German Shepherd named *Kebaio*. He and his wife are passionate about art, although neither is particularly artistic in their own right. They purchase works from living artists; and only ones they meet personally. He and his wife travel to shows and galleries specifically to meet new artists and experience their work firsthand. When asked why he collects only living artists, he replied, "Rembrandt, Cezanne, and Picasso are long gone. Purchasing their work benefits only those with the good fortune and bank accounts to own them in the first place. They are merely commodities. I buy from the artist directly. I feed and support them and their dreams – and not some broker sitting in a back room somewhere. We end up with great art and wonderful friends to boot." High Q people always seem to have a good reason for *everything* they do!

Like most Europeans, Heinz is an unrelenting and unapologetic foodie. My gastroenterologist tells me he eats to live, but doesn't live to eat. He's never met or hung out with Heinz. Heinz has turned eating into performance art. Heinz and his wife celebrate the people in their lives with as much vivacity. One Friday afternoon an impromptu gathering broke out at Heinz's place. The group included government officials, a few actors, a poet, several artists, one model, two farmers, a chef, two garbage men, a wine sales person, a shopkeeper - and me among others. Each person had one thing in common – they each loved and lived life! Impressed with the diversity of Heinz's friends, I once asked how all of these people found each other. He replied, "That's the magic of life. Passion befriends and embraces those who invite it into their life."

DEMANDING MORE IN A HIGH Q LIFE

Life is simply too short for mediocrity and accepting what everyone else takes for granted. Think about your life and define the standards by which you live it. Demand more. Expect more. Become more.

Setting exceptional standards is an interesting, yet somewhat challenging process that everyone should undertake. Once you begin thinking about your world and everything in it, you are likely to become upset at the way some people and companies treat you. Good for you! This is where your life strategy of valuing yourself, integrity, and the power of relationships come together to form something quite intriguing. Being in a true position of power means having the ability to say, "*No!*" When you demand more, you walk in the room with the freedom to walk out. Never miss an opportunity to steer others away from a bad experience. Neither should you miss an opportunity to steer someone toward exceptional relationship opportunities.

When you encounter someone or a company who treats you poorly, walk away. Don't waste your time letting them know why you won't be patronizing them in the future. Let them figure it out on their own. However, never fail to let everyone you know about your experience. When someone in government treats you poorly, do the same thing – but also add your representatives and the media to your mailing list.

Seek out and embrace those people and companies who treat you exceptionally well. Let them know you appreciate them. Let your family, friends, and colleagues know about them. Everyone appreciates a tip for a great resource and the relationships you develop will serve you well for years and perhaps decades to come. Just ask Heinz!

Demanding more isn't simply a person-centric activity. It touches every relationship in your life. Demanding more means demanding more quality and integrity with the food you eat, the places you visit, and the people who share your life. It's also about supporting the good in the world and walking away from the bad or substandard. Demanding more is about valuing those things that provide value to you and your life. If something falls short, it has no place in your life unless it can meet your expectations and standards.

Expecting and demanding more from yourself benefits you and your quality of life significantly. Sitting down, exploring, and developing standards within your own life is something all should do, but few ever accomplish for one reason or another. Like most, I had loosely applied standards, but most weren't particularly formalized. Even with my own standards, I applied them rather selectively and experienced mixed results because of it. I've established serious and consistent standards for myself today, and stick to them voraciously. I ultimately learned the remarkable power that the ability to say "no" truly offers – and I love it!

Establishing higher standards by which we expect to be treated is something we should all do as young adults. By setting the standards for your life, you are not only rewarded with the power of "no," but also an abundance of exceptional people, places, and things that add unparalleled value and contribute generously to the quality of your life.

One of the first standards I established addressed the companies I patronize. I decided not to do business with companies that use predatory practices, employ fraudulent strategies, are deceptive, or harm consumers and societies. When it comes to demanding more from the companies I work with, few areas are more fraught with peril than banking and finance.

I've known many in the world of finance and banking throughout the years. I've also learned many of the games that are played every day, and the infuriating way companies treat their customers. I decided not to risk my money where the odds were decidedly against me, the rules were merely suggestions for the most part, law enforcement efforts and oversight are haphazard, largely overlooked, and wildly underfunded, and those in leadership roles encouraged and allowed people and societies to be harmed so they could profit. Instead of supporting predatory companies and their practices, I now bank at credit unions where my money doesn't feed the huge salaries and the often-surreptitious business practices.

As far as investment is concerned, stocks and bonds are no longer options in my portfolio with a Wall Street and financial system that's lost its sense of shame. Today, I invest directly in projects and private ventures. The risks associated with America's current financial culture are not ones I want associated with my portfolio, future, or life. My returns are safer, more ethical, and far more lucrative than what I could ever expect from Wall Street – at least without being an insider or a congressional representative.

Some of my standards, however, are not so grandiose. My first and foremost is one I call my *Platinum Standard*. It tells the world and reminds me that any standard I apply to others I will apply equally to myself. This is my most important standard.

It can be a challenge to begin establishing formalized life standards that are wrapped around expecting more. To get you started, here are a few of mine.

- *My Platinum Standard* - Everything I expect from others I expect from myself.

- I simply don't tolerate or participate in *mediocrity*.

- If any person, company, or government *treats me or anyone else with anything less than total respect or integrity*, I will not associate, patronize, or work with or for them.

- If any person, company, or government *displays a lack of integrity or does not respect others*, I will not associate, patronize, or work with or for them.

- If any person, company, or government is *dishonest or is deceptive*, I will not associate, patronize, or work with or for them.

- If any person, company, or government *uses divide and conquer tactics, or Machiavellian strategies,* I will not associate, patronize, or work with or for them.

- If any person, company, or government *uses others for their own gain without consideration for those people*, I will not associate, patronize, or work with or for them.

- If any person, company, or government *discriminates in any way (legally defined or not) that inhibits any one's rights to the pursuit of life, liberty or happiness,* I will not associate, patronize, or work with or for them.

- If any person, company, or government *lies to others or me,* I will not associate, patronize, or work with or for them or the company they represent.

- …and *many* more.

You may first see standards as something that limits the people, places and things in your life. However, one of the most powerful and important functions of standards is to include only the best people, places and things in your life. **Setting standards is very much of an inclusionary process.** This is a life strategy with remarkable and exciting potential. You're telling the world that you only associate with exceptional people, places and things. Anything or anyone less need not apply.

Another powerful impact of demanding more from life is that as we apply higher standards, the best and brightest rise to the top! We remove much of the power of deep pockets and corruption from our lives and make them less important along the way. When enough other people do the same, such entities will eventually lose the fuel they require to exist.

In a Nutshell

Demanding and expecting more in and from life is a quality control and gate keeping function with powerful benefits. It's not an arrogant or self-centric experience. It is about increasing the quality of your life and reinforcing it with quality relationships that contribute positively to your life experience.

Inspiration

You are exceptional and important. Demand respect. Demand dignity. Demand honesty. Demand integrity. Demand quality. Demand to be treated as the valuable person you are – and demand that those you know and patronize treat others the same. High Q people demand more from the people, places, and things they include in their world – and they get it! It's just that simple. Heinz is a great example of how demanding more from everything around you changes life profoundly. There's no reason for you not to experience the same remarkable lifestyle.

Set your standards high while defining yourself, everyone, and everything that is part of your life – and never deviate or make excuses that subvert or diminish those standards. By defining exceptional standards, you protect your world and your quality of life.

Practical Life Design Strategy

Let's define and explore your life design a bit more closely.

16.1 Why does a society that accepts and tolerates mediocrity suffer?

16.2 Why do companies that offer mediocre or substandard products and services survive?

16.3 Who commands this relationship: one who demands more or one who offers less? Why?

16.4 Do you characterize yourself as someone who accepts less or demands more?

16.5 How do you believe life standards would change your life?

16.6 Develop a list of at least 15 quality standards for your life.

16.7 If you were to develop a strategy to design your expectations of people, places, and things in your life from this point forward, what would it be?

CHAPTER SEVENTEEN
STANDING

"Life isn't about what you say you are. Nor is it about what you are against. It's about who you are, what you do, and how you relate to the least around you. It's about what you're for."

~ **Ian Breck**

One of the most powerful, empowering, and sexy characteristics of any individual is found in their beliefs. It's not about being heard. It's about becoming a voice for something greater than yourself. Standing for something is an exceptionally healthy behavior, and something that every High Q individual I've ever met embraces.

Standing for something is more than casting your opinion and voice upon the masses; that's showboating. It's about sharing your knowledge, expertise, experience, influence, mentorship, and voice in ways that get others thinking and talking about those things that make our world a better place to be. As part of a high quality life, it's not an option; *it's a responsibility.* And anyone who understands it will tell you that it's also an overwhelming gift.

Contrary to popular belief, standing *for* something doesn't necessarily mean standing *against* anything. Once you sit down and think about it, standing against something isn't particularly creative, valuable, or even constructive in the grander scheme of things. In fact, it often comes off as cheesy, trite, and ignorant. Those who know me understand my contempt for corruption, greed, predation, and fraud. However, being against these things is nothing more than stating the obvious. It offers no particular original thought, value, or intrinsic expectation of change. It just makes me noisier than you – at least for a moment. Being against something is probably more deeply rooted in our desire to express and be heard than it is to effect change.

I learned long ago that there are far smarter ways to skin a cat – and be happier with the differences made along the way. It begins by ending all expectations that anyone else will make a difference. Many people complain about the world today, but few ever take their displeasure any further in most cases. If you truly believe in something, you have to be willing to make a difference through your behaviors - and not simply your voice.

The challenge is to rearrange your thinking. As opposed to standing against corruption, predation, and fraud, I stand for ethical, honorable, and responsible business practices. It's a difference with a powerful distinction. As it turns out, what it is that I stand *for* provides me with a far more compelling voice than what I would otherwise have if I stood *against* something.

Standing for something demands more than an opinion and loud words to communicate your position. It requires you to weave your beliefs into the fabric of your life. Standing *for* something is a behavioral feature of your lifestyle. It's also about leading by example. Because I value quality companies so highly, I don't do business with those that employ dubious or predatory business and/or personal practices. Throughout my years as an executive, what I've stood for has meant hundreds of millions of dollars in revenues for great companies. It's also meant the same in losses for lesser, more unsavory ones. In addition to supporting quality companies, I also became empowered with the differences and statements I was making socially.

One of the great misconceptions about standing for anything is the idea that you must necessarily stand against something. This simply isn't true. You can stand for anything you're passionate about ranging from ambient music to woodpeckers, safe food, theater, rug tying, dogs, or even responsible crab trap construction! That's the beauty of it – it's your choice and there are no limits or rules.

More importantly, being for something doesn't necessarily mean that any particular injustice has to exist. You can stand for something simply to bring attention to it. Just remember that whatever you stand for must be backed with actions and behaviors that advance your cause and contribute to its betterment. That's another beauty of standing for something – it's about making the world a better place to be one passion at a time instead of just bitching about it like everyone else!

The world can be a truly unpleasant place, and there are no lack of contentious issues that come along with it. However, the world still contains so much more good than bad. Sometimes, you simply have to look more closely to discover it amongst the fog of the news, self-absorbed special interests, and even reality television! I stand passionately for integrity, ethics, the arts, the environment, and protecting those things that are still great about our world and deserve our appreciation and protection. It makes my day so much brighter and more welcoming than getting up annoyes because another fool is up to his or her usual lunacy.

STANDING FOR SOMETHING IN THE HIGH Q LIFE

I'm often asked about how I've had the opportunity to meet the many High Q people I know. Despite having a career where I've had the privilege to know such people, I've met many through friends, events, gatherings, sailing, and photography. It was at one such gathering when I gained a particularly interesting insight into how many High Q people end up in the careers they do.

It was a wonderful balmy June evening just outside of Stony Brook, New York on Long Island. I was invited to an evening with friends at their beach house on the Sound. It was a small gathering and I knew several of those who would be there and looked forward to catching up.

The evening was perfect in terms of weather and ambiance. Cerulean skies covered light glistening sands, smells of gourmet food, and muffled laughter as discussions of the day's events continued briskly and unchoreographed. Several frolicked along the shore. I was being introduced to what seemed to be hundreds of people – each with an interesting story of their own. One was a book collector, a music professor, a Michelin-rated chef, a wine merchant from Brooklyn. Each had a name, career, and a fascinating story. I admittedly find it intriguing why people select the vocations they do. This evening it seemed as if the entire gamut of people had come out to commune under the stars.

As the evening progressed, a music professor entertained us with his gift of rare celluloid jazz standards that somehow fit perfectly in the scene. I sat in an Adirondack chair nestled somewhere between sandy shores and the gentle periodicity of Long Island Sound, where my toes swished through the briny cocktail of tepid water while discussions and wine ebbed and flowed.

The group I was with was an interesting cross-section of society. One was a tunnel engineer for the Metropolitan Transportation Authority in Manhattan, a priest, a professor, an entertainer, a playwright, a composer, a chef, an organic farmer (a husband and wife team), and me, of course - a knowledge engineer.

After several glasses of wine and various stories, my curiosity finally got the best of me. "So," I asked, "what makes people select the careers they do? I mean did you suddenly turn eight and decide to be a priest? Did you tell your friends in school that you've always dreamed about being a tunnel engineer? And, what, pray-tell, makes anyone want to be a professor?"

The priest popped up first, held his wine glass high and replied, "For me, it was the endless supply of mediocre but acceptable Pinot!" Everyone broke out laughing. However, each eagerly went through their stories of how they arrived in their profession. As the stories unfolded, patterns began to emerge. Each had a specific reason for their particular career choice. For the priest, it was about changing the face of a damaged church. For the music professor, it was about introducing people to "new" old, but nonetheless important music that has been overlooked in an otherwise commercialized industry and culture. For the chef, it was about introducing interesting and healthy foods to locavores. For the tunnel engineer, it was about creating tunnels safer than the one that cost his father's life. The organic farmers wanted to bring quality and reasonably priced foods to people who could not otherwise afford them. For the playwright, it was about giving people a new way to see and experience their world. My personal decision was based on my desire to reveal the otherwise nebulous world of knowledge and expertise so that people could become more engaged with their lives. Interestingly, our careers were all driven by our passions, beliefs, and ultimately what we stood *for*.

That night was one of the most truly wonderful evenings I have ever experienced. By the end of the evening, I had been introduced to an amazing array of new friends, and insights that I still value today.

That night I also learned that standing for something can take on many forms and offer unparalleled benefits. Virtually all High Q people I've encountered have a profound reason for their career and almost every other choice they make. Passion and purpose tend to make better and more impassioned employees, and quite remarkable advocates for professions, employers, and ultimately, themselves. I can also tell you that a gently inebriated priest is so much funnier than you would ever expect.

In a Nutshell

Standing for something certainly has a welcome place in our society. However, in the terms of a high quality life, it offers even more compelling benefits with the potential to increase your value as an individual through an empowered sense of wellbeing, and also by being a more powerful voice that is guiding society to a better future.

Another key feature related to standing for something is that it offers you an exceptional opportunity to mentor and share your knowledge and expertise with people around you.

Inspiration

Your life gains invaluable direction, value, and meaning when you stand for anything – whatever that may be. It defines you in a positive light both to yourself and to others in your world. You can stand for one thing or many things. There's no limit or rules to hold you back. Just remember to make what you stand for part of a lifestyle, or your victory will be hollow.

As you weave your beliefs into your life, your voice becomes far more authoritative and carries so much further in the winds of change.

Practical Life Design Strategy

Let's explore what you stand for in your life.

17.1 List the top five things that you are against in life.

17.2 When thinking of each item you listed in question 17.1, identify why you have the position you do.

17.3 When thinking of each item you listed in question 17.1, list what you do to stand against each item in terms of behavior and lifestyle.

17.4 When thinking of each item you listed in question 17.1, how would you turn what you are against into something you are for?

17.5 List the top five things that you stand for in your life.

17.6 When thinking of each item you listed in question 17.5, identify why you have the position that you do.

17.7 When thinking of each item you listed in question 17.6, list what you do to stand for each item in terms of behavior and lifestyle.

17.8 If you were to rate yourself in terms of the quality of an advocate you are for on a scale of 1 (lowest), and 10 (highest), what would your score be – and why?

17.9 If you could "rearrange the furniture" of your advocacy, what would you do to make your life and the world a better place to be?

17.10 If you were to design a strategy about what you stand for in your life and how you will accomplish it from this point forward, what would it be?

CHAPTER EIGHTEEN
LOVING DEEPLY

"A kiss; what a brilliant distraction that ends all discussion and allows the voices of our hearts to sing."

~ **Ian Breck**

Love – what a concept! I mean, what is this thing that causes our innards to flutter and our brain to cast away its reasoning and logic? Although I find myself engulfed in its wonder and power from time to time, I often find myself at a loss when it comes to describing what it really is about love that is so awe inspiring and attractive to everyone. Something tells me I am not alone in my wondrous ignorance.

Love has been defined as:

1. A profoundly tender, passionate affection for another person.

2. A feeling of warm personal attachment or deep affection, as for a parent, child, or friend.

3. Sexual passion or desire.

4. A person toward who love is felt; beloved person; sweetheart.

5. A term of endearment, affection, or the like.

Love is the perfection of passion. It's the ultimate manifestation of life. I can love anything, or I can love nothing. However, what would life's purpose be without loving something? A life without love implies an existence devoid of attachment, intimacy, and passion. A life without love makes life all but meaningless. We are creatures designed to love and be loved.

Love in the High Quality life

Love adds amazing beauty to life. However, love is not only important for a quality life, but also has a profound effect on your health. Experts are now discovering that love, sex, and friendship provide invaluable health benefits that range from faster healing to coping with chronic illness more effectively. Love may also help you live longer.

Studies conducted at the University of Pittsburgh reveal that women in happy marriages demonstrate a substantially lower risk of cardiovascular disease than their less matrimonially inclined counterparts. The National Longitudinal Mortality Study that has tracked more than a million people since 1979, says that happily married people live longer, have fewer heart attacks, less disease, and lower cancer rates.

The benefits don't stop there. The University of Iowa reports that female patients with strong personal relationships benefit from greater activity of natural "killer cells" at the site of ovarian cancer tumors.

If hot and steamy sex is something that is illusive in your life, no worries. Hugging, or simply sitting close to someone you care for, can reduce your blood pressure and also increase your production of the stress-relieving substance oxytocin that plays an important role in orgasms. In fact, frequent hugging throughout the day may lower women's blood pressure as much as 10 mm/Hg thanks to increased oxytocin production! For men, the news is not so good, however, the steady diet of sex that hugging often invites, tends to even the score between the sexes.

So, is sex really that good for you? Absolutely! Studies show that men who have sex at least twice a week decrease fatal heart attacks by more than half. Frequent ejaculation also appears to offer some degree of protection against prostate cancer.

There you have it. Loving and its related behaviors have absolute health benefits and advantages. Nevertheless, what are the benefits of other forms of love? If wild monkey sex isn't in the cards this week, what do you have to look forward to in terms of life and life quality benefits? As it turns out, lots!

The hobbies and activities we enjoy are terrific stress relievers, can increase our self-esteem, and sense of accomplishment. All of these things have powerful health benefits and contribute significantly to life quality. Studies show that "loved" activities have significant potential to reduce the influences of depression and anxiety, while providing one of the most powerful developmental activities children (and I suspect adults) can perform. The elderly benefit from mind-building thinking games, which studies show may help delay the onset of Alzheimer's and dementia.

The benefits of loving are simply too many and too deep to include in any book. If you're skeptical, however, a simple search of the Internet will turn up multitudes of studies that are revealing the remarkable power of love, loving, and living. You will become a believer in no time. The power of love, hugs, simply holding hands, along with activities you are passionate about, not only increases the quality of your life, but also possibly the length of it!

High Q people embrace love in all of its forms and make it a part of their daily routine. It's not simply something they benefit from; it's something they share with others. That's why it's so common to see High Q people greet each other with hugs, kisses, and frequent "I love you's." When I visited Heinz in Switzerland, almost every shop we visited began with the ubiquitous hug, pecks on the cheeks, handshakes, and sincere welcomes that made each experience exceptional - and further reinforced the relationships that each valued so highly. Loving deeply is truly a win-win situation for everyone - and a wonderful lifestyle enhancement to boot!

So, what if you haven't found that special person in your life yet? No worries. Fill your life with the things that you love like activities, foods, hobbies, pets, or whatever - and love them deeply! You will be amazed at the people who will notice this remarkable characteristic about you. Loving the things in your life deeply is one trait very few individuals of any appreciable value don't find uber-appealing. I think you might be surprised how loving life alone rewards you.

Loving is an essential element of the quality life. Let's explore a few areas where High Q people find inspiration, love deeply, and share that love with others.

Crafts

Crafts and other creative endeavors are wonderful opportunities to take a break from your world and pamper yourself. Many studies suggest that even simple crafts reduce heart rate, lower blood pressure, and can reduce the impacts of anxiety and depression.

When it comes to crafts in the lives of High Q people, the world is their oyster! From personalized gifts and holiday decorations to exquisite art that draws exceptional prices, crafts and works of art are common elements of a high quality lifestyle.

Gardening

Gardening is an exceptionally popular activity among High Q people – and not just because they're voracious foodies with an appetite for the finest and freshest foods! Along with reducing stress and anxiety, gardening influences life quality positively in terms of its inherent beauty, growing healthier foods, reducing financial expenses, and a host of other benefits. Plus, most people simply love the activity, sharing, and exploring amazing new ways to enjoy the fruits of their time and labors!

Pets

The research findings are undeniable: pets reduce stress, provide companionship, increase lifespan, and are essential elements of virtually every high quality life I've encountered and explored to date. Dogs are the favorites because of their unconditional companionship, intelligence, and love. Cats follow in a distant second place. Hamsters edge out fish for third. Birds round out the top five most popular pets.

If you have the desire, ability, sense of responsibility, and can fit one or two into your life, introduce yourself to your new fuzzy, feathered, or scaled companion. You'll be a better and more interesting person because of it, I promise!

Photography

As a collected fine-art photographer, photography is my most immersive and undeniable pleasure. I first ventured into photography as a child to escape the world. Throughout my life, however, photography has evolved and advanced to a highly artistic endeavor. I conduct workshops, and consider photography a deeply rewarding and wonderful excuse to get together with friends, family, and colleagues. Photography is truly a remarkable part of life that has made my world a better place to be.

As it turns out, photography has many benefits from both mental and physical perspectives. Photography offers a wonderful artistic outlet that provides a sense of accomplishment and a wealth of benefits. When traveling, photography provides me with an opportunity to explore my world, and is also a source of exercise. When you combine these benefits with the wonderful social interaction, it's easy to see why the popularity of photography has boomed in recent years and continues to grow.

Photography is also one of the most intriguing and expressive of the arts, and is available to virtually everyone today thanks to digital technology. Whether as an artistic pursuit, hobby, or a reason to interact with others and explore the world, photography has earned a profoundly special place in many high quality lives today – including mine!

Sports

If you want to release some pent-up steam and reset your day, nothing works quite like sports. In high quality lives, sporting events are commonplace. Whether it is all out sports like racquetball, volleyball, stunt flying, or basketball, or less aggressive forms like cycling, bowling, curling, softball, or shuffleboard, sports release tension, make you feel better physically, reset your mind, and provide wonderful opportunities to stay fit and interact with others regardless of your age.

Sailing keeps my mind sharp, provides an awe-inspiring escape and an exceptional opportunity to share my time and experiences with family and friends. Golf, on the other hand, makes me want to drive my car into a tree! However, I still enjoy it immensely and keep refining my divots despite the anguish! Regardless of who you are, your age, or what you enjoy doing, an entire world of sports is out there just waiting for you to become a part of it. Finding a sport that suits your lifestyle, age, social requirement, and activity level is sure to provide a welcome addition to the quality in your life.

By the way, doctors are now telling patients to get off their butts and get active! As it turns out, *activity* may be the secret ingredient of increased health and longevity.

Music

Jim Moeller, well-respected owner of Serenity Music (SerenityMusic.com), and I were talking one day about the substantial influence that music provides listeners. He noted that music is one of the most powerful psychological stimulants known, and that we're just beginning to realize its potential in areas of psychology, medicine, life, and life design. It's true. Music has the power to transform mood, alter emotions, and change the way we think. It also stimulates production of a variety of chemicals within the body.

A great deal of research is being conducted concerning music's capacity to influence both physiological and psychological states, as well as providing tangible rewards that advance healing and benefit chronic disease. Retail stores, offices, and answering machines have employed the power of music for years to make us relax, become excited, and even induce spending. In the end, music is a powerful psychological influence you can leverage to your advantage.

With music's ability to redefine or enhance people's mental states, it should come as no surprise that High Q people tend to use it extensively within their lives. Whether for ambiance, or as the driving force behind a party, romantic interlude, or just to enhance their attitude, High Q people commonly acknowledge "engineering" environments with music. It's also an activity that you should explore a bit more on your own.

Reading

Few activities open more windows than reading. Every High Q person I've met considers reading an essential part of living well. Whether you're a fiction fan, or prefer to spend your time learning, or exploring, reading offers limitless possibilities to take your mind in new directions and keep it sharp along the way.

In a Nutshell

These are only a few examples of making the things you love a part of your life. Obviously, there are many more. Regardless of your personal diversion, filling your life with the things you love offers unparalleled benefits and is a fundamental activity within every high quality life.

Inspiration

Loving is an important psychological and physiological feature with the potential to impact the quality of your life significantly. As a "reset activity," loving allows you to relax, escape, and reset your mind. It also provides a remarkably powerful grounding mechanism that reduces anxiety, stress, and stratification.

While not all of the benefits of loving will ever be known, the ones we do know about today offer compelling views into the potent differences that love and loving make in the quality of every life today.

Practical Life Design Strategy

Let's explore loving deeply in your life.

18.1 List up to ten (10) things you absolutely love, or love to do that ARE a part of your life today.

18.2 List up to ten (10) things you absolutely love, or love to do that are NOT a part of your life today, but you would like to include.

18.3 What are your favorite activities and how often do you do them?

18.4 When thinking about question 18.2, how could you integrate these activities or interests within your own life?

18.5 How does loving deeply relate to relationships?

18.6 How does loving deeply relate to passion?

18.7 How does loving deeply relate to dependence?

18.8 How does loving deeply relate to valuing yourself?

18.10 If you were to design a strategy about how you will include, grow, and nourish more love in your life from this point forward, what would it be?

206 | **Reimagined**

CHAPTER NINETEEN
THE LEARNED

"Learning isn't an age thing – with the exception that it keeps the body, mind, and soul young."

~ **Ian Breck**

This is one of the shortest chapters in this book – and yet one of its most profound. Three of the most important things you can do for your life (and the world) are to grow, feed, and nourish your mind. It's that simple. In the first few chapters of this book you discovered that knowledge is the foundation of life and living well. It should come as no surprise that your life and how you live it are made possible by and with the knowledge you possess. When you stop learning, processes begin that result in the deterioration of not only your brain, but also your quality of life – and in many cases, your independence.

Lifelong learning is a conspicuous hallmark of every high quality life I've encountered. It's common to see High Q individuals taking college courses in their eighties and beyond, or throwing pottery at a local class. In the final analysis, it doesn't matter what you're learning, it matters only that you are encountering new ideas and exercising your mind with whatever turns you on. Lifelong learning nourishes and rejuvenates your mind - and also your life.

The benefits of lifelong learning are truly compelling and exciting. Aside from the obvious benefits, an active mind may lead to a healthier life in later years. In addition to making us more valuable social voices, helping us adapt to change, and introducing us to new social networks, lifelong learning is also a powerful activity that helps us feel better about our world and ourselves.

Lifelong Learning in the High Quality Life

Most experts agree that lifelong learning, when integrated fully into your lifestyle, contributes substantially to life quality, overall happiness, and your sense of wellbeing. The great thing about lifelong learning is that it can be accomplished in so many ways.

Here are a few ideas you can weave into your life to make lifelong learning an important and continuing element of your quality life pursuit.

Read!

Reading books and magazines that expand your knowledge is a wonderful way to keep your mind active and more reactive throughout life. The subject isn't important as long as you read it. The activity of reading itself is what makes the real difference when it comes to a sharper and healthier mind.

Keep a "To-Learn" list

I love this idea. Identify those things you want to learn about and list them! Then start learning your way through your list!

Spend more time with intellectual friends

As it turns out, knowledge is contagious! By interacting with intelligent people, you hone your knowledge and cognitive skills along the way and also learn through various viewpoints.

Take a course

Many colleges and schools offer courses for adults and some even allow you to "audit" courses (not for credit) for free or at greatly discounted rates. However, taking regular courses offers credits and potentially a new piece of paper for your wall!

Learn something fun and new

You can find any number of courses for activities from crafts and sports to vocations and fine art appreciation that can expand your artistic and social horizons. Look to museums and organizations for educational programs as well.

Make education a core part of your life's experience

Make the commitment to take at least one course every six months or so, and visit museums and exhibits often. It's affordable, opens new windows, makes you smarter, is healthy, and won't make your butt look big! It might even expand your sphere of friends! Speaking of which, why not get a friend to come along with you?

Teach

Many people are surprised to learn that one of the most powerful forms of learning is teaching! Share what you know with others and help them refine their own knowledge and expertise under your expert tutelage. It's rewarding, satisfying, and keeps you exposed to new ideas and people.

Collaborate

Getting together with others to produce, teach, learn, or do something new is a remarkable way to learn, and interact with others in an exceptionally healthy way.

Discover a job that challenges you

It's simple: if your job doesn't stimulate you, find one that does. Society is filled with people who have transitioned from lifeless jobs to new careers that change their life quality abundantly.

Just do it!

As it turns out, *doing* is also an exceptional educational activity. Get together with friends and experience something new together. It doesn't matter if it's cooking or kite flying! Not only does it challenge you, but it also allows you to develop valuable expertise that is both deeply rewarding and highly satisfying.

Go beyond your traditional limits!

Look at doing something you would never regularly consider doing - at least once a year. Try skydiving, ballooning, or scuba diving! Go beyond the traditional confines of your own life to experience and discover what's in store for you out there! For an even better time, share your new experiences with your friends!

Break barriers in your life!

This is all about new activities in your life. If you have never been interested in bluegrass or country music, go to a concert and become immersed in a truly remarkable experience. Why not get your PhD. in basket weaving or pottery? Even better, volunteer and simply share your time with someone who needs a friend for a while.

Get even smarter!

If you love cooking, try culinary courses! You can always be better at what you love – and being better is better for you!

Write a book!

Writing a book isn't for everyone and it's certainly not a simple endeavor. That being said, it offers wonderful opportunities to share ideas and reach out to special people just like you!

Lifelong learning is more than an idea. It's a strategy that makes wonderful differences in your life. It's also something with the potential to make your life an even more amazing and satisfying place to be.

WHERE IT FITS

Learning is a profound activity with a multitude of benefits that includes keeping your brain alert and at its best throughout your life. Learning exercises the brain and mind – and it's every bit as important as physical exercise to happiness and creating a life where you thrive.

From a health and life quality perspective, learning is heavily associated with stress reduction, relaxation, social behavior, interaction, and self-awareness. These behaviors alone represent remarkably powerful and compelling reasons to make learning a part of your life every day.

Inspiration

Your life is defined and shaped by the knowledge you provide it. Knowledge is brain food. Learning not only exercises your brain and mind, but also nourishes your life and contributes significantly to its quality. Make learning a central strategy and maintain a commitment to learning more and making your life a much more amazing place to be!

Practical Life Design Strategy

Let's explore where continual learning can fit into your life.

19.1 What do you do to increase your knowledge on a continual basis?

19.2 What would you like to do to increase your knowledge and expertise, but have never taken the time to do?

19.3 How often do you visit museums, or other educational activities?

19.4 What expertise do you have that you could teach others? Have you ever considered such a pursuit? Where did it lead?

19.5 You can learn by being taught, teaching, and doing. Which technique best describes you?

19.6 What is your favorite activity – and have you ever taught it to anyone else?

19.7 How many books do you read a month – and what are your favorite genres?

19.8 What is your favorite genre of television programming?

19.9 When you watch educational programming like that found on the Discovery Channel®, TLC®, The Science Channel®, the History Channel®, or the like, do you listen to learn, or just have it on for background sound?

19.10 How many classes or courses of any type do you take annually?

19.11 When is the last time you took a course or class?

19.12 If you were to design a strategy about how you will incorporate learning into your life from this point forward, what would it be?

CHAPTER TWENTY
LIFE'S CURRENCY

> *"The activities in your life produce the qualities of your life. Choose them wisely."*
>
> ~ Ian Breck

From the very moment I became interested in high quality lives, I noticed a common thread among the people - they always seemed to be doing something. They were like ants in a colony. I joked with colleagues that High Q individuals made me feel lazy and uninspired at times. As it turned out, for High Q people, activity is something more than merely a task – it drives their lives.

Activity is to life is what exercise is to health for High Q people. It doesn't matter how large or small the activity; it matters only that it focuses your attention on something you enjoy. The activities in our lives are the lenses through which we experience and relate to our world.

If we could peer into the High Q mind, we would discover that High Q individuals see their world differently than the rest. They see it in a more emotional and interactive way and tend to experience life more deliberately. To High Q people, life is not a series of tasks to be completed; but a series of people, places, events, and things to be experienced. This single point of differentiation sets High Q individuals apart from all others.

The high quality life experience is about the experience of life itself. High Q people see activity as the beginning of something more to come. It's not a party, but an occasion to interact with others. It's not a vacation; it's an exploration and chance to experience new places. Life is so much more than merely activity; it's about the experience of the world – and making the resulting qualities a part of your life.

However, what truly makes activity the currency of the High Q life is that High Q people aren't simply active; they take it one step further.

Activity in the High Quality Life

As I was exploring the various ordinal strategies that drive quality lives, I realized quickly that these strategies were ostensibly the same for all people, with the exception that High Q people built them into their behaviors and lives more completely. While this answered some questions, others remained. I couldn't get it out of my mind that High Q people somehow seemed different with how they approach life. It wasn't a good or bad thing. It was a *different* thing. They were usually happy and at peace with themselves and life in general. Everything seemed to be in order within their lives – perhaps a bit too much in some cases. I was missing something.

One day I was having a less than stellar day when I met with a High Q friend for lunch. She asked how I was doing and I kind of rolled my eyes and told her that if today were a fish, I'd throw it back! She laughed and commented that when she felt down, she liked to walk around Hermosa Beach when she's in Southern California, or Sausalito when she's up north. If it had been any other day, her words would have been banal conversation. However, after months of banging my head against why High Q people's lives seemed so ridiculously orderly, one person's words of wisdom became my epiphany. I tossed my head back and exhaled a huge sigh of relief and sat there clapping like a retarded seal after realizing I'd just discovered the missing link. Life works out that way sometimes; the gods occasionally smile upon retarded seals!

If activity provides the qualities in our lives, and life is influenced by the qualities specific activities provide, why can't we tailor our activities to the life qualities we want to experience? I wish I could tell you this is original thought. However, High Q people commonly design their lives around the qualities they most want to experience – and have been doing so forever. High Q people engineer their lives more than others do. This is a distinctive behavior that High Q people exhibit - and also the missing link I was looking for.

I have to admit that the idea of experiencing life in such a way was a stretch for me at first. However, that's how I believed the people I was trying to understand saw their world. Now all I had to do was substantiate it. That proved to be a cat with different stripes.

When I first had an inkling and considered the idea that High Q people see and experience their world through engineer-colored glasses, I didn't bring it up to my colleagues for quite some time in fear it would make me sound goofier than I already did at times. However, I finally broke down and presented my observations and theory for their consideration. They thought I was nuts! However, they also entertained my wistful thoughts and theory nonetheless – probably out of sympathy. (Did I mention that I signed their checks? It's good to be king.)

I decided the best way to explore my theory was to replicate the experience of living a life designed exclusively around specific responses from activities. It's not often when you have an opportunity to experience your own theories in action through a firsthand account. I wasn't exactly sure of what I was doing, and quite frankly, I doubted it would achieve much of anything. However, I realized that, if I could replicate just a small part of the experience, I could perhaps learn a great deal from it. Besides, my sailboat was involved. How bad could it be?

I'd scheduled a few weeks off to do some sailing in New England. My last vacation was three years ago. I needed a break and had just purchased a sailboat and wanted to shake it down a bit before setting sail for Bermuda a few months later. I sailed into Port Jefferson, New York on the north shore of Long Island for a few days. Having lived in Stony Brook some years earlier, which is just down the road a bit, it gave me an opportunity to catch up with a few friends.

Unlike visits of the past, this weekend would be different because it was designed deliberately to yield specific life qualities I wanted to experience. I wanted to experience a typical relaxed East Coast weekend. I also wanted warmth, inclusion, joy, comfort, contentment, the unhurried East coast vibe, camaraderie, and perhaps even a bit of competition to spice things up a bit. I set out first to identify the specific activities that would make these qualities possible.

Instead of meeting friends at their homes or the local watering hole as had been my modus operandi in the past, I planned the weekend around spaces, places, and activities specifically selected for environment, ambiance, and their return of specific qualities. My first concern was that my plans might simply transpose our usual experiences to new locations. You know, a "more of the same in a different place" kind of thing. Nonetheless, I'd designed a progression of events that became the stage for whatever came next.

An important note to make is that my weekend was designed using an organic core strategy. I sought only to provide the foundation for what would happen next. It is exceedingly important that you leave a place for life to grow and happen.

I picked up my mooring, secured my vessel, and made my way ashore. My friends, Rob and Carolyn, met me and we were off to dinner with friends in Stony Brook. As we drove down Christian Avenue, I couldn't help but be taken aback by the picturesque verdant green foliage and the charming background that frames Stony Brook's quaint "downtown" area. I used to take it for granted when

I lived there. I mentioned this to Rob and he agreed, having moved away before returning with his wife several years later.

We arrived at the restaurant and met in the bar for a quick drink and the ubiquitous welcoming hugs and pecks before dinner. The ambiance added an unexpected dynamic to the experience - and to the entire evening for that matter. Once dinner was done, I invited everyone back to the boat for a nightcap. Normally, we then would've called it an evening and headed home.

Everyone made it aboard and experienced an amazingly beautiful late spring evening as only New York can serve it. I look back at that night and realize the inspiration behind those amazingly produced San Pellegrino "*Live in Italian*" commercials that I still can't seem to get out of my mind. (I would expect no less from *Ogilvy & Mather!*)

Evening became late night, and then spilled into morning. I awoke to seven sprawled bodies scattered throughout almost every conceivable nook and cranny of the boat. As each came to life to the wafting aroma of Tarrazu coffee and the scent of the freshly-baked blueberry and cranberry muffins I had picked up earlier, I offered to have them all join me on a weekend sail to Sag Harbor in the Hamptons. After making last minute arrangements, all agreed excitedly.

The cost for the trip was a competition of sorts. Knowing we had two professional chefs on board, the two choose team members and were tasked with creating a dinner on each of the two days we would be gone. The winner would be crowned, "Best Chef in the World!" They had about three hours before we would set sail to design their meals and provision. It was kind of like Project Runway for foodies, except this time it ended up being men against women. That's just how life happens on the high seas.

As everyone headed to the farmers, meat, and fish markets for provisions, I straightened the boat and headed to the bakery and wine store up the street. I become stuck in a Filliniesque vinophile's pornographic dream at a local wine shop that had me mesmerized with a truly spectacular selection of wines – all of which I wanted, of course. Luckily, I only had time to grab a few bottles, several loaves of bread (challah, baguette, and a few other brownish grainy-looking things) on my way back. I remember thinking how nice - and different - this weekend was turning out to be. Life was good – just add water!

Once everyone had returned, we set sail for Sag Harbor. The trip was brisk and lively which made it seem much faster and even more engaging than it already was. The company was perfect, and a continual stream of delectable hors d'oeuvres rolled through the companionway as one chef tried to outdo the other. (Chef's take competitions very seriously, and we used that to our advantage!) That night we passed the Sag Harbor breakwater as the sun slipped below the horizon and dropped anchor. We ended the evening with an inspired dinner, wine, laughter, and a well-earned sleep beneath the twinkling skies of the Hamptons.

I awoke the next morning to glints of sun through my eyelids, seagulls "singing" as they flew overhead, the smell of the salt-entrained ocean - and the constant clang of a halyard rudely slapping against the mast of a sailboat whose owner obviously had no idea of etiquette. This morning, however, two of our crew had beaten me ashore for coffee and sticky buns. That was perfectly fine with me.

I had no special plans for the day other than simply experiencing life with friends in Sag Harbor. We spent most of our day drinking and eating our way through the former historic whaling village and playing around the water. One hour lead to the next - and then to the next. It was simple, elegant, wonderful, and time passed all too quickly. The dinners each evening were spectacular and the weekend ended all too soon. As everyone left to return to their busy lives elsewhere, I remember feeling alone for a brief moment.

The next morning, I sat barefoot in the cockpit with my cup of coffee and reheated day-old sticky buns thinking about the weekend. I realized this weekend was unique from any other I had ever experienced. Every moment was uniquely meaningful and rewarding. Had I been a screenwriter, I would've walked away with the inspiration for my next award-winning project. Even years later, my friends still comment about our time together.

That weekend was one where I learned several things about life, living – and, yes, even myself. The first was that, given the opportunity to do so, life develops and blooms beautifully on its own; it simply needs the freedom and a stage on which to do so. By taking only a few moments to set that stage with an eye toward the qualities it will return, the experience of living becomes significantly more vibrant and profound – maybe even to the point of being a bit overwhelming at times. I also realized, in a rather melancholy moment, how much of my own life I had squandered simply by not realizing, or at least taking the time to explore the many truly wonderful ways to experience it. When it comes to living life, you can be a passive observer, or hop in the driver's seat as your designer. There really is more than one way to experience life. The choice of which is yours to decide.

Throughout the next few weeks, I sailed to Cape Cod, Martha's Vineyard and Nantucket with various friends joining each leg of my journey. I continued to design activities around the responses I sought so eagerly to experience, and simply allowed life to happen.

Friends joined me to fly kites at Katama Beach on Martha's Vineyard. We walked the shores at Edgartown at dawn looking for shells and whatever else had drifted ashore with the tide. We rode the famous Flying Horse Carousel and grabbed the brass rings at Oak Bluffs, and enjoyed a bonfire with wine and marshmallows on Nantucket that lasted until morning. None of the activities were expensive, but all were exceptional. I discovered the transformation from everyday to breathtaking required only thinking a bit differently about the world you experience.

In retrospect, my experience was far more than I could have ever imagined. My weeks spent at sea that spring and summer were beyond my wildest expectations in terms of experience alone. I watched life unfold far more beautifully than I ever expected possible. I simply had to think in terms of activities and their qualities. It's admittedly different and definitely takes a bit of getting used to. However, it's also something that's eminently doable and becomes easier with experience.

My single greatest take away was that activity for the sake of activity isn't particularly useful or fulfilling. The idea is to create a backdrop where life can unfold, and then simply allow it to do so. In the end, it's about laughing and even sometimes crying together or by yourself. It's about chemistry and humanity blended with the perennial wonder of the world. It's about moments reserved for you and your thoughts, or you and the thoughts of those around you. Sometimes, it's just about being alone in your own little corner as the world whizzes by blindly. Perhaps my greatest discovery was that an amazing life isn't a control thing - *it's a letting go thing.*

The idea that one can design their life around activities and the responses they return sounds a bit robotic and possibly even new age at first. I understand those sentiments completely. However, when you think about it and experience it for yourself, becoming more creative with your life is an absolutely mind-boggling experience with almost miraculous results. If you want to live your life well, simply add some creativity, impulsiveness, a dash of sharing – and some thought. Once I experienced it for myself, I realized all I had missed throughout a life focused on a career and discovering the next "big" thing. I ultimately discovered the biggest things were actually the smallest.

In the final analysis, designing your life is about designing the activities that shape and define it. It's also about concentrating the qualities that are most important to you into your life. It's bringing together the people, places, and things of your life and setting the stage for life to happen on its own. It always does – and far better than if micromanaged or plotted out meticulously.

Perhaps now you can understand why I believe that activity truly is the currency of life.

In a Nutshell

Despite experiencing lives filled with activity, we rarely consider how those activities contribute to the quality of our lives. While we may design our lives from a task-based perspective, we rarely take into consideration what certain activities contribute precisely, and how we can design specific qualities into our lives. I now understand how and why High Q people savor the moment from the scent of a flower to the magic of life at the beach. It starts by simply being there.

We tend to become locked into our daily routine. While routines offer predictability, it's often at the cost of opportunities to experience life and the world differently. A simple impromptu picnic with a few friends or a loved one at a park can transform a regular day into a spectacular one. Deciding to visit somewhere new and taking pictures to add to your home is another great idea. Perhaps it's camping for the first time, or cycling through a forest that may be just the things that pique your life juices. Are you ready for curling lessons? Even a trip to the zoo can reopen old worlds and new experiences. Regardless of the activity, what you fill your life with is what defines your life and its quality profoundly. Design your life amazingly! Design your life around what and whom you love and what you love to do – along with the qualities they introduce into your life. The world's a miraculous stage on which life is experienced. *Become creative with it!*

Inspiration

Designing the activities within your life by paying greater attention to what they provide in terms of life qualities compels you to evaluate activities more closely and pay greater attention to detail and purpose. Reimagine and discover the qualities you want in your life, and explore and design into your life those activities that provide them. It's a wonderfully healthy exercise in both life design and editing – and something that is a unique element in the high quality life.

Practical Life Design Strategy

Let's explore a bit more about the activities within your life.

20.1 List at least 7 activities you enjoy so much, or that add to the quality of your life so substantially that you could do each at least once every week.

20.2 List at least 7 activities you don't enjoy, or that detract from the quality of your life so substantially you could do away with them and have your life become a better place to be.

20.3 When thinking about question 20.1, list how each activity makes you feel personally, and why it contributes to your quality of life.

20.4 When thinking about question 20.2, list how each activity makes you feel personally, and why it detracts from your quality of life.

20.5 Thinking about tomorrow, write down what activities will occur (one per line) from the moment you wake up.

20.6 Thinking about question 20.5, rearrange your activities to introduce at least one (if possible, two) items from question 20.1, then live your day according to your new schedule.

20.7 When thinking about your day (after you have experienced it) according to the activities you scheduled in question 20.6, how do you believe your changed influenced the quality of your life that day?

20.8 For the next week, schedule your days with an eye toward how your activities influence the quality of your life. After experiencing your week, how would you say the changes you made influenced your life and its quality?

20.9 If you were to design a strategy about designing the activities in your life - and how you will accomplish it from this point forward, what would it be?

CHAPTER TWENTY-ONE
HOW IT ALL WORKS

"It's not the structural design of your life that matters as much as the engineering behind it that tells the true story."

~ Ian Breck

So, there you go! Now you know what drives exceptionally satisfying and rewarding lives. As my research was concluding, I sat in front of my fireplace with a glass of wine and a piece of paper. On that piece of paper was a list of rules and strategies that define and control who we are and the lives we experience. I thought to myself that this was what my career had boiled down to – a rather anti-climactic single page of scribbles. Perhaps the most disconcerting part was the fact that these strategies were ones everyone possesses. It wasn't like any of these items involved super powers like flying in a single bound, ESP, or walking on water as I had once expected. My grandmother, friends, and colleagues possessed these things. However, what made them so different for High Q people? As it turned out, that was like wondering what makes the recipe for Coca-Cola® special.

From basic understandings of knowledge and how we use it to core strategies that provide foundational rules and more focused strategies used to deal with the nitty-gritty details of life and living, each of us possesses a distinct collection of tools that not only makes life and living possible, but also defines who and what we are and the quality of our life experience. The difference is that High Q people don't simply understand each strategy; *they build them into their lives and life experiences.*

So, how do you know when your life design is well designed or at least "good enough?" The ultimate metric of success in terms of life design and quality is simple: *contentment*. Regardless of who you are, what you do, your passions, career, or the life you live, your sense of contentment is the canary in the coalmine in terms of life design and quality. If you've designed your life well and are living it based on your design and terms, your sense of wellbeing will be good, and you will experience an overwhelming sense of contentment.

In the final chapters, we'll begin taking the ideas from the pages of this book and introducing them into your life.

Let's create a happy canary!

Section Three - Life Design

You know more about knowledge. You also know about the people who live quality lives. Now it's time to put your knowledge to work in your own life.

Welcome to Life Design.

Important Caveats...

- **Reimagination is a process that should only be undertaken by *mentally healthy* individuals.** If you are under the care of a health professional, make sure you consult with them about your plans before embarking on any reimagination effort.

- **You're the gatekeeper of your life.** The final decisions for changes to your life are your responsibility alone. If you are uncomfortable with a potential change, or are unsure if it's appropriate, don't do it! Speak with trusted friends, family, or competent professionals to ensure you're doing something that will not harm you, or anyone else.

- **Reimagination requires total honesty and integrity.** It's your life. Being dishonest instantaneously taints and ruins your efforts. You'll never outsmart yourself or your life.

- **The reimagination process takes place one step at a time.** Always make sure you complete one step before continuing to the next.

- **Even if you only want to tune your life up,** always start with a blank slate.

- **Take notes** throughout your experience and refer to the notes you've already made in your Life Journal.

- **Reimagination is not an instant or overnight process;** that's not how it works. Reimagination makes many small changes over time as opposed to larger changes at once. This allows you to undo changes that don't fit well, refine the ones that do, and ensure a smooth landing as new lifestyle patterns begin to emerge and integrate with others.

- **Modify your life plans as often as necessary,** but give each modification the opportunity to "take hold" before tossing it aside because you're not noticing results yet. Results take time to "set" in your behaviors and life.

- **Having a friend, family member, or colleague join you** can provide huge benefits, an important counterbalance, and a far more engaging and explorative experience.

- **Have fun!** Reimagination should be a stress-free experience, although it can be challenging and will definitely have you thinking along the way.

CHAPTER TWENTY-TWO
PUTTING IT ALL TOGETHER

"Stop talking, planning, and dreaming. Get off your excuses and create the future you've always talked about, planned for, and dreamt of!"

~ **Ian Breck**

This is where everything comes together. You're about to discover the true coolness of reimagination. The idea behind everything you've done to this point has been to create the foundations that a quality life requires to exist, grow, and thrive. However, have you figured out how the pieces all fit together? It begins with one important bit of knowledge about high quality lives: There are only *five* things you can accomplish with your life in terms of greater meaning and satisfaction.

A Quality Life's Five Basic Activities…

• You can design, create, and live a life that *attracts* and invites wonderful people, places, and things into your life.

• You can *convert* the finest people, places, and things in your life into trusted and valued elements of your life.

• You can *retain* those people, places, and things that make you and your world a more special and interesting place to be.

• You can reap remarkable benefits and rewards from a life well lived when others and the relationships within your life *advocate* you and your wonderful example to others.

• You can *leverage* all five life activities to *explore, discover, and be inspired* by the people in your life and the world you share.

These five things start and end with a quality life. Acquiring a high quality life begins with taking the responsibility for your own life, how it's designed, created, lived, and the outcomes associated with your design. You must also be committed to protecting your life from those things that take away from its designed intent. The responsibility to elevate both you and your life to their true potential is ultimately yours.

Understanding the nature of knowledge and expertise allows you to make wiser decisions, create smarter solutions, and solve problems more accurately. These also empower you to be smarter, maintain control, and define and protect the life you've always dreamt of living.

By learning more about the strategies that drive those who experience quality lives, you've gained invaluable insights into the foundations of happy, content, and satisfied people. Develop soil that a quality life requires to grow and thrive.

When everything comes together, you have what's required to support and allow the positive changes to come into your life that enable it to thrive. The stage is now set for you to grow a far more satisfying and meaningful life.

GET READY...

One of the greatest challenges to a successful reimagination has nothing to do with the process itself - it's about you: *impatience*. As you begin reimagining your life, you'll naturally want to speed things up a bit to see what happens when all of the cool changes you've worked so hard to develop get up and running. Other people adopt more of a "mix-and-match" strategy where they try to combine multiple strategies thinking they're outsmarting the system. They're not. While I applaud and embrace enthusiasm, you simply can't outsmart your own brain. As amazing as it is, it has limitations. Shortcuts ruin the reimagination process.

Reimagination demands you make only *one* strategic change at a time in your life. This is the *single-step approach*. One reason for this approach is to avoid something called "life shock," which occurs when you introduce sudden or significant changes to your lifestyle over short periods of time. The consequences can be considerable and often result in frustration, anxiety, depression, and the failure of your plan along with the associated loss of confidence and willingness to change your life because of your fears of failure. Keep it simple and reimagine your life design one step at a time.

Another important argument for the single-step approach is that it allows for testing of new ideas before introducing them into your life. This is not only the smartest way to ensure what you're doing is best, it also offers an opportunity to refine your understandings, strategies, models, and scenarios along the way when things don't go as you expect them to.

Finally, when you introduce more than one strategy into your life simultaneously instead of allowing each to become established individually, they tend to become entangled with each other. The result is like pudding that doesn't set up properly; what's left is unappetizing and useless. This practice not only confuses and corrupts life strategies, it also often destroys the integrity that strategies share and require with each other.

It's important to remember that High Q people don't suddenly become who they are overnight; it's a process that requires years. Your advantage is that you understand more about the process, which tends to compress time. This fact alone will undoubtedly make you want to speed things up a bit by virtue of your wonderfully human nature. However, be aware of your nature and remember the costs of exuberance.

As you begin making new ideas part of your life, keep in mind you're also introducing new sets of rules and strategies to be used within your life. Your life doesn't always play well with new ideas. Your mind is used to the tried and true rules and strategies it uses every day and won't necessarily embrace change and your newfangled ideas at first. Your real self is funny that way. Your old rules have become highly compiled elements of your behavior are pretty much automatic – which is just fine as far as your brain is concerned. New rules require a conscious effort to override existing behaviors – at least for a while. However, once you begin integrating new strategies into your behaviors, positive results begin appearing and Mozart and your inner self's eventually adopt your new strategies quite nicely.

Once you introduce new changes to your life, you will begin noticing results almost immediately. This is your life and brain responding to something new and exciting. It's critical to listen to your mind, understand what it's telling you, and discover why it is telling you what it is each step of the way – both good and bad. Listen to it. Refer back to this book and your notes often. You can also visit IanBreck.com for additional resources or to ask questions you may have. If the results of your changes are different from what you'd anticipated, discover why and determine whether it's your expectations that are flawed, or that further refinement of your ideas may be in order. Give your new life changes an opportunity to develop and mature. Like wine, they get better with time! Give each step the time it requires to become an exciting new part of your life.

Essential Considerations

You are your life's designer and gatekeeper. This means it's you who has the final word on the changes that are introduced into your life. If you make a mistake or are uncomfortable with your results for any reason, STOP! Explore your strategy and understand why you are experiencing a different result than what you expected. Then, explore it further. Are you using a synthetic or organic strategy appropriately? (Remember, they cannot be mixed!) Are you using correct decision strategies? Are other life strategies adversely influencing your results? Are your expectations appropriate? Are you creating your own set of reimagination rules? Ask lots of questions, refer back to this book, your notes, and explore your problem with trusted friends or family to try to understand what is happening before continuing. Only once you've resolved any conflicts or misunderstandings should you continue integrating further changes into your life and lifestyle.

Finally, have fun! It's so exciting to improve your life - and it's even more so when you're your own designer!

GET SET!

Your first step is to revisit each chapter in *Section Two: Life Strategies*, and begin integrating the lessons from each chapter into your own behaviors and life. Address each chapter in Section Two using the following steps:

- **Explore and refine each life strategy within the context of your own life.** What do they mean? What is it telling you? What's your take on the ideas presented? Do you agree or disagree? Why? Try to understand the underlying principles and adapt them into your own life. Explore the concepts with others. Make each your own.

When you've developed a good grasp of each chapter, write down what it means to you within the context of your own life. It can be a paragraph or a book. This is the process of formalizing your understandings.

- **Next, it's essential to remember that it's not enough to understand a life strategy – *you have to live with it*.** Design your new life strategy into your life and behaviors and how you live. Explore imaginative ways to integrate your new life strategies into your life.

In this step, make a list describing at least ten ways to integrate the life strategies into your behaviors and life. This is your *action list*.

- **Implement your action list for at least *three* weeks before continuing to the next strategy.** Many people prefer to acclimate to new changes for at least four weeks. This allows them adequate time to refine and allow their strategies to set properly.

Many report that exploring their new understandings and life strategies with friends or family goes a long way toward helping them gain fresh ideas and perspectives.

Remember, *it's not a race!* There are no time limits or expiration dates involved. Take your time and explore each strategy. Keep in mind that it took you this long to get here in life; it requires time and effort to move you toward an even more amazing you. Be patient! Be thorough! Be deliberate! Be amazing! It's your life. It's your opportunity!

Go!

The chapters in *Section Two* are not laid out in any particular order of importance. The only exceptions are the *Relationships* and *Dependence* chapters, which should be explored in the order presented. Otherwise, feel free to explore and immerse yourself in each chapter in any order you wish.

Typically, I suggest *Valuing Yourself*, as an ideal starting point to get you up and running. Many people simply follow the chapters in order. The choice is up to you.

Reread each chapter and make sure your understandings and strategy haven't changed from when you first completed the questions at the end of the chapter. Re-answer the questions – especially the last one! Review and refine. Review and refine. Review and refine. Create your action list and begin integrating your new strategies into your life.

As you begin reshaping your life, note the changes taking place within your life in your Life Journal – especially ways you might tweak things a bit to exceed your expectations. Few changes are perfect on paper or in the mind – and that's actually a good thing.

In most cases, my clients typically set aside at least *one month* to work on and integrate each new strategy. This allows immersion to occur and enough time to experience and refine the changes they have adopted. Some people prefer even longer periods for their changes – especially for more complex strategies like relationships. Take the time you need to get it right.

As you continue through the rest of the chapters in *Section Two*, you will begin noticing rather profound life changes. If the changes are good, make them a part of your life and enjoy what they introduce to the experience. If not, stop and rethink your strategies. With each new strategy comes a new set of qualities in your life. Experience and embrace the great ones – and realize they will remain for as long as you provide a place for them to thrive.

240 | **Reimagined**

CHAPTER TWENTY-THREE
LIFE DESIGN

"If you want to improve your life, start with its design, then live that design passionately!"

~ **Ian Breck**

The idea that we might be able to reimagine and redesign life is an idea that has intrigued me for years. The thought of having greater control over how we live and experience our own lives is truly a fascinating proposition when you think about it more closely.

Each of us lives unique and meaningful lives. However, more often than not, the design of our lives becomes dictated by reality and happenstance rather than the dreams that were once so clear in our minds. You're about to learn how to redesign and write a new chapter to the most amazing book in the world - your life.

It's time to bring your experience full circle and explore the possibilities of… well, *you!* It's time to assume your intended role as your own life's designer. In this chapter, we'll explore the process of redesigning your life.

Before we begin, I want to start with an underlying thought. Go into this exercise understanding that you're truly a wonderful person with a great deal of value to yourself, others around you, and the world. You deserve and were designed to experience all of the amazement that life on this ridiculously amazing little blue ball has to offer. You are only here for a short time in the grand scheme, and the things you do, the people you include in your life, the decisions you make, and how you choose to experience your life are destinies only you should control and define. The life you live today creates the memories you carry throughout the rest of your life. Take responsibility for your life and live it beautifully. Dance with your dreams, design the stage on which you play, and embrace everything "you." It's your life. Live it amazingly!

The world's truly a better place with you in it. It's time to make the world a better place *because* you're in it!

Reimagining the design of your life begins by simply thinking about it – *but differently*. The final stage of the reimagination process prompts you to explore and try on several *"what-if"* lifestyle scenarios. You'll start by creating several *life designs* or *life models* as we call them.

STEP 1: STOP!

Reimagining your life begins by first thinking about what your life would look like *if it were lived differently*. From your career and where you live, to your social life, passionate pursuits, and even personal relationships, reimagination gives you an opportunity to play around with the furniture of your life a bit while exploring what a few changes might look like. If you like the changes, work toward making them a permanent part of your life. If not, toss them out and start again.

Life reimagination begins with a blank slate – well, sort of. It's more about how you would change your life from this moment forward. I've found that one of the best tools for reimagining your life is a simple sketch. It doesn't have to be pretty or perfect. It's simply about exploring the "what if's" in your life.

So, where do you start? First, get a pad of paper. (I prefer larger sized sketchpads and Sharpies® myself). The choice of your media is entirely up to you; just keep lots of it on hand!

The next step is to begin simply. I advise my clients to start their design with a single activity they would like to live their life around, and then build their life design from there. For most, that particular activity is something they love to do, or something they would like to build a life around. This activity becomes your *defining concept*.

Let's assume that have a passion for fine art oil painting. If you build your life and career around oil painting, what would your life look like? What would you have to do to market and sell your work? How would you support yourself as a painter? What would your average day look like? How would you deal with responsibilities? As you begin answering these questions and filling in the blanks, you begin creating what we call a life model.

Life models are nothing more than simple sketches created to illustrate the key concepts of your life and living. It can include as many or as few details as you prefer. When starting, keep the number of details lower until you become more familiar with the process. Your only big decision is where to begin, and even that's about to become much easier!

When creating life models, there are two basic styles to choose from. The first is an *activity-based* model, or more simply, an activity model. As its name implies, this model allows you to design your life around activities that are important to you.

The second is a *quality-based* or quality model. This model focuses on specific life qualities that are important to you, and the subsequent activities that provide, reinforce, and sustain those qualities. I advise most to start with an activity model and progress to quality models.

The Activity-Based Life Reimagination Model

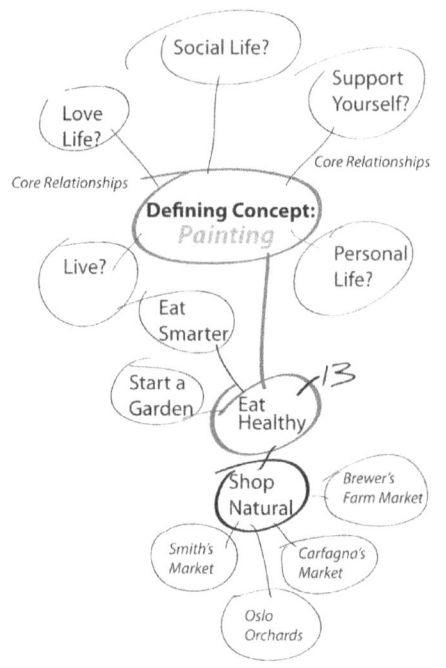

FIGURE 23.1 ACTIVITY-BASED LIFE MODEL

Figure 23.1 illustrates a very simple activity-based life model. It's easy to create and simple to understand. It begins with one primary activity that you would like to base your life around. This becomes your "*defining concept.*" In this case, it's *painting*. It could just as easily be motherhood, nursing, or training squirrels to fly.

Once you've determined your defining concept, describe the critical (*core*) relationships you would have to consider if you decided to build your life around painting, or whatever your defining concept is. *Core relationships* are essential to life and living, and commonly include essential features of your life like children, spouse, etc.

In this example, core relationships include personal, love, social life, eating healthy, income, and where you'll live once you're an artist. Add as many core relationships as desired or needed to bring clarity to your life model. Or, you can start with the most important ones for now, then add the rest later if you decide your model has wings and you want to detail it further. If a particular core relationship is already present and acceptable in your life, don't necessarily expand it, but include it as a placeholder.

Next, select a core relationship, explore it and expand on it. In this example, this person chose eat healthy because that's an important change they want to make in their new life design. At this point, simply sit back and explore each core relationship more thoroughly. What are you going to do to support your core relationship? What can you do to allow it to thrive?

> **Note:** *In Figure 23.1, you will note the number "13" linked to the **eat healthy** core relationship. This helps you to layout your strategy for eat healthy on another piece of paper, if you prefer. Generally, I lay out major activities on the main page, and detail each on separate pages. I also use this system to create multiple possible strategies for an activity. In this case, I might design four or five strategies for eat healthy and name them 13-a, 13-b, 13-c, and so on.*

As you can see in Figure 23.1, this individual wants to eat smarter, start a garden, and purchase natural and healthy foods to support their goal of eating healthier. The selection of "shop natural" has been expanded to include some of the food markets that can help satisfy these requirements. This shopping scenario might be integrated to create a regular shopping day alone or with friends.

The further you break down any element of your design, the more detail it reveals. It's important not to break your activities down to a super-fine level, however. Leave room for life to occur.

This process is repeated with each core relationship in your model. Once complete, you will have successfully outlined what your life might look like from a 2,000-foot-high perspective. As far as the minute nitty-gritty details are concerned, don't worry about getting too detailed. Add only enough detail to outline your plan to an understandable degree. If you decide to use this model down the road, life will present many opportunities for you to fill in the blanks.

The activity-based model is a great way to explore the possibilities of a life based on a significant activity, interest, or passion – which describes the dreams of most people. The key to the success of this model, however, is to select one overriding activity to build your life around. If you have more than one activity you would like to explore, build a model around each and merge them later. Your activities can be defined as narrowly or broadly as you wish.

The activity-based life is also a fascinating exploration and a fun exercise that allows you to explore the possibilities of your life if it were lived differently. The overarching object of this model is to get you to think more critically about potentials and dependencies associated with them. My clients absolutely love this model and use it often. I believe you'll enjoy it as well.

The remarkable popularity of the activity-based life model is due in large part to its ability to illustrate life possibilities easily and in an orderly manner. The major weakness of this life model is that it doesn't address specific life qualities that might important to you. To correct for this, this model must be *balanced* after initial design has been completed. We'll learn more about this later. (See "*A Balancing Act*" later in this chapter.)

So, what do you do if you want to design your life around core qualities like love, adventure, and passion instead of a specific activity? If this describes you, a slightly different approach is required.

THE QUALITY-BASED LIFE REIMAGINATION MODEL

In the activity-based model, we explored life changes in terms of the activities within our lives. The quality-based model visualizes life in terms of *life qualities* you want as a part of your life. This model is particularly useful when you want to build a life of specific life qualities, and the associated activities that provide them.

In the quality-based model, life becomes the defining concept as opposed to a specific activity. In the example below (Figure 23.2), we start by listing several life strategies that are important to the defining concept of "*Your Life!*" In this example, we've included a few of the life strategies that High Q people share. (For brevity, several are omitted.) The life strategy of independence is expanded upon.

FIGURE 23.2 – THE QUALITY-BASED LIFE MODEL

The quality-based life model emphasizes desirable life qualities, and the subsequent activities that provide those qualities. It is an advanced model that requires a bit more attention to detail. However, the strength of this model is that it allows you to define your life around the qualities that are most important to you. The weakness of this approach, however, is that it doesn't take into account the activities that are truly important to you unless those activities happen to return the same qualities you're seeking. As you might expect, when incorrectly applied, this model can develop into "a tail wagging the dog" situation if you're not careful.

In our example (Figure 23.2), being more independent is an important life strategy for this individual. The quality is expanded and explored further. We break independence down into major areas and define the key activities that can make greater independence possible. In this case, financial independence has been broken down further. To address the need for increased income, activities like "painting" and "consulting" have been added to support the requirement of increased income. It's a relatively straightforward approach.

This model is an excellent tool to explore the life qualities that are important to you, and to define what provides them. It's also a wonderful way to explore how activities often contribute unexpected combinations of qualities within your life.

So, Which Model Is Better?

Each model is different; neither is superior to the other. I like and use both models depending on the situation, and application. I sometimes use both. Most clients focus on the activity-based model for the general layout of life models. They then apply the quality-based model to explore important qualities they desire in their lives such as intimacy, self-sufficiency, etc. later in the process. When each model has been completed, you'll have a pretty good idea of the requirements and an outline of the life you've dreamed of living.

You'll discover quickly that it's easy to end up with five to ten (or more) different activity models and even more life quality models. This is how it's supposed to work. Most people find that quality models help them explore life according to their passions. As you get toward the end of the process, your quality models should all fit neatly into, or at least be compatible with, your activity models. Once this occurs, you've successfully created a "stable" life model.

As you get started, you'll discover reimagination is a remarkable process with the power to reveal countless fascinating nuances that potential changes may reveal in your life. It will make you think – and it won't happen overnight. The process requires intense thought to reach a successful conclusion. However, once your life model is complete and stable, you'll know and feel it immediately!

Models help clarify ideas about life and living, and provide invaluable maps for successful efforts. I spend a great deal of time modeling with my clients because of the enormous value models provide in terms of discovery, clarity, planning, revelation, and exposing critical and missing elements of life and living well.

Sage Advice

Life modeling is a deceptively simple, yet highly profound process that reveals life's details through the interactions between your mind and the realities of your life. It allows you to explore your life through new and exciting lenses. If your reimagined life design doesn't work out the way you expected, simply toss it out and start over again! It's not a race, there's no right or wrong, and there's no score keeping involved. That's the beauty of moving the furniture of your life around a bit before actually committing to anything permanent.

Keep your models reasonable and practical – even if it requires a bit of work on your part to accomplish elements of your life design such as additional education, or perhaps a new employer. The idea of being the world's hottest new novelist is possible if you're willing to put in the required effort. However, imagining your life as king or queen of Outer Slobovia won't mean much if you don't have royal blood to begin with, and no meaningful links to the throne.

The idea behind life modeling is to create an idealized version of your life based on who and what you are, what you enjoy, are passionate about, and what you love. Explore your ideal job, relationship, partner, daily routine, events, and more with an eye toward your passions, interests, and what excites you. As you reimagine the details of your life, modify your life model accordingly, and note important changes or thoughts in your Life Journal along the way.

Don't edit your existing life. *Start anew.* This doesn't mean that many of the things in your life today can't be included in your reimagination. However, it's far better to start anew and discover what emerges from an unfettered exploration.

When reimagining your life, don't forget to include "*hard*" realities like children, family, and things like existing health issues and other realities of your life. "Soft" realities include things like your career, home, spiritual beliefs, and even your partner. These are more negotiable. Remember, very few rules exist in life. Use this to your advantage!

A common question I receive from clients and readers alike has to do with someone else assisting you in your reimagination effort. Outside of a joint participant, like a friend, partner, or colleague, the answer is "*no.*" You really don't need anyone's assistance if you follow the guidelines in this book. If you prefer a more personalized and detailed experience with professional mentorship and direction, please visit IanBreck.com for more information.

Finally, I cannot emphasize it strongly enough – reimagination doesn't and shouldn't happen overnight! It's designed to provide a series of well thought out smaller changes in your life as opposed to life-shocking massive changes. Take your time and get it as close to right as possible.

A Balancing Act

Reimagining and modeling your life is a wondrous and free-thinking exercise - to a certain point. It's important never to forget the ultimate idea behind reimagination and modeling is to discover a quality life. It's essential to ensure your new life design delivers the life qualities you most desire. To see if your life model design meets your requirements, "*balancing*" is performed on the models you create. This is only necessary with the activity-based life model, but some also balance their quality-based models for good measure.

Once you've defined your new life model to a point where you're ready to consider implementing it in your life, the next step is to "balance" it. This process ensures the qualities you most desire in your life are present and accounted for in terms of your life plan. Because activities produce qualities, balancing desired activities against your desired qualities ensures a lifestyle model that includes the qualities you most desire in your life. Balancing your models requires an existing life model design – and a red Sharpie!

How it's Done...

Balancing a life model starts by defining the qualities you want expressed in your life. Make a list of the qualities you want in your life (Figure 23.3), and then compare those qualities to those of your life model. If your life model doesn't include a particular quality that is important to you, modify it accordingly.

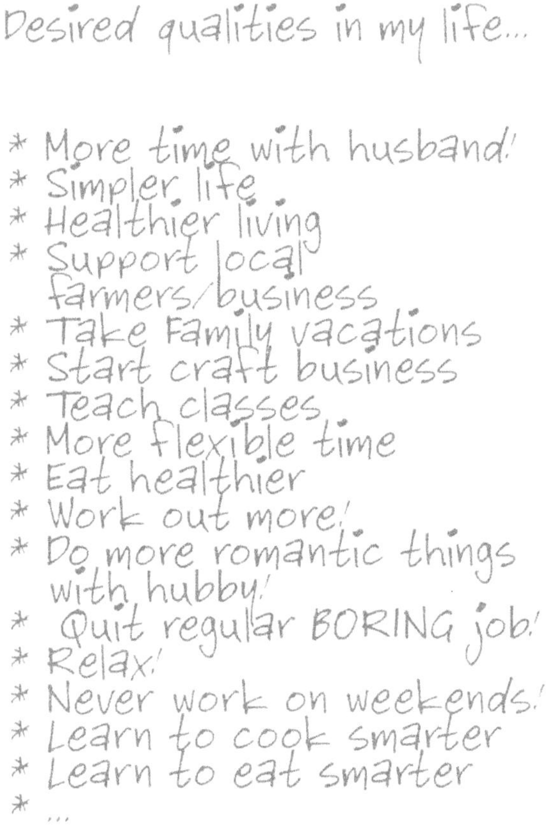

> Desired qualities in my life...
>
> * More time with husband!
> * Simpler life
> * Healthier living
> * Support local farmers/business
> * Take family vacations
> * Start craft business
> * Teach classes
> * More flexible time
> * Eat healthier
> * Work out more!
> * Do more romantic things with hubby!
> * Quit regular BORING job!
> * Relax!
> * Never work on weekends!
> * Learn to cook smarter
> * Learn to eat smarter
> * ...

FIGURE 23.3 – DESIRED LIST OF QUALITIES IN YOUR LIFE

Here's a simple quality list. Make sure that you include all of the qualities important to you in your list. Many people find they have to come back several times to add new qualities as they think of them.

In the next illustration (Figure 23.4), a simple way of balancing an activity-based life reimagination is illustrated.

FIGURE 23.4 – BALANCING YOUR ACTIVITY-BASED LIFE MODEL

In this example, asterisks (*) illustrate the qualities that result from each activity. Ideally, these qualities will match the list of qualities you defined in your life described in Figure 23.3. If a quality is missing or different from your model or *life quality list*, explore and adjust your model or life quality list accordingly.

LIFE 2.0

"*Life 2.0*" is what I call the final reimagined version of your life. Your life 2.0 scenario consists of the best tidbits from all of the life models you've created. The numbers of life models you create are limited only by your imagination. The more you have, the greater your opportunities will be to draw from each and add to your ultimate life 2.0 *scenario*.

To ensure you have the greatest possible understanding of each life model you create, answer each of the following questions to the best of your ability and include your answers with each life model you develop.

23.1 What is the primary activity in your life you wish to be defined by, and why is it so important (what does it provide) to you?

23.2 When thinking of question 23.1, how could you extend and enhance your life experience through supporting activities?

23.3 Describe the people in life 2.0, and what each contributes to your life and its quality.

23.4 Describe your career in life 2.0, and what it contributes to your life and its quality.

23.5 Describe your typical day in life 2.0, and how it contributes to your life and its quality.

23.6 Describe what about life 2.0 makes it special and exceptional to you.

23.7 Describe what makes life 2.0 different from your current life.

23.8 Thinking of your answers in questions 23.1 through 23.7, please list the qualities that each answer introduces to your life.

23.9 From a life quality perspective, how do you want to feel emotionally in life 2.0? Please list each quality, as well as a brief description of each.

23.10 In question 23.8, you listed the qualities that your activities introduce to your life 2.0. In question 23.9, you described the qualities you want to experience in life 2.0. Do both lists match each other?

23.11 If the qualities you want in your life (question 23.9) are different from the ones that your favorite activities introduce to your life (question 23.8), how can you modify life 2.0 to make both lists match?

23.12 Based on your answer to question 23.11, what would you have or do to make life 2.0 practically possible?

In this simple exercise, you are further defining the ideas that drive your life models. In most cases, I advise clients to create at least *five* different life models to draw from. The more you have to explore, the better your scenario will be.

Creating Your Life 2.0 Scenario

Once you've defined your life models to your satisfaction, it's time to create a life 2.0 scenario using them. A life 2.0 scenario is a super life model that contains the best ideas from the many life models you've created. *A life 2.0 scenario is always activity-based.*

For your defining activity, select one activity that is most attractive to you and make it your defining concept.

Once you've defined your life activity, add your core relationships by selecting the best ideas you've explored from each life model you've created. What are the best possible income sources, career choices, and places to live? As you continue to build your scenario, borrow the best from your life models to complete your scenario. As it becomes more complete, you will start reimagining how all of your relationships fit together and begin discovering the new life you are designing.

Evaluating Life 2.0

Once you've developed your life 2.0 scenario, it's time to explore it in greater detail. Remember that your life 2.0 scenario is only a *rough* guide. However, it sets the tenor and provides the basic outline of your *idealized* life.

Take a few weeks, or however long it takes, to explore and evaluate each area of your life according to your life 2.0 scenario. Try each on for size. Imagine "a day in the life," and see how everything feels and works together and make the necessary tweaks along the way. Is it possible? What would it take to make it a reality? As you continue exploring and reimagining, continue filling in the blanks with details you perhaps forgot or failed to consider, and continue refining your life 2.0 scenario.

Once you've explored the possibilities of your scenario and have detailed it to your satisfaction, you are about ready to start putting your life 2.0 design to the ultimate test – *taking it live!* Don't worry - you can still change your models and scenario at any point. Just remember, we're still in the design phase of the reimagination process – everything is still editable and possible.

What an exciting place to be! You've gone through one of the toughest exercises of any new life – *reimagination*. Most people love this process after they get started and tend to come up with several plausible life scenarios. That's the magic behind the entire process. However, it's something that takes a great deal of thought and some time to complete. It's your life – it's worth it!

The Final Step

Once you've designed and created your life 2.0 scenario, it's time to decide whether to put it into action. If you like and are ready for what comes next, congratulations!

To turn your life 2.0 scenario live, start with addressing core relationships first – *one at a time*. It's important to ensure you've accounted for each core dependency associated with your defining concept first. If one relationship is dependent on another, make sure you address your core relationships in the proper order. If you have missed any details, complete them and ensure they are accurate before continuing.

To make your process easier, create a life model for each core relationship you have, and outline it and its dependencies just as you did with your life models. Once you're satisfied with the design, begin making the changes.

After completing the first core relationship, move on to the next one, and so on. Once your core relationships have been addressed, you should be in the perfect position to begin experiencing and making your defining concept part of your life!

Welcome to your amazing new life!

CHAPTER TWENTY-FOUR
AFTERWORD

> *"Life is about connections. It's about relationships. It's about decisions. It's about vision. It's about living. Mostly, however, life's about loving the life you're living."*
>
> ~ **Ian Breck**

I think back to the seemingly endless days and nights I spent wishing I had shared more of what I've learned and made more of a difference for other people. I was simply afraid I'd run out of time. As evidenced by this chapter, thankfully that wasn't the case.

In our final days, we experience something called *twilight clarity*. This is a special state of existence where we can look back on our lives with perfect clarity and understanding. It's always been my dream to shift twilight clarity ahead in life to a point where we can still do something about the life we see, and experience the enormous benefits it offers a bit longer. I believe this book can help you do just that.

I want to leave you with an insider's glance of what those potentially final days revealed to me.

People are overwhelmingly good and kind. Each deserves the opportunity to live an amazing life according to their own terms and should be encouraged in both voice and spirit by all others who want the same for themselves.

Regardless of how hard you work, how smart you are, or whom you know, luck plays a pivotal role in life. The objective of a life well lived is to place yourself firmly in the way of luck.

The only "lesser" individuals in society are those who believe they are superior to others. They are merely fools. Never give one an audience.

Most of the bad in the world is caused by a relatively miniscule number of disgraceful people. The only people more disgraceful are those who do nothing about them.

The earth is an amazingly beautiful oasis in the cold vastness of interstellar space. Yet, we treat it as if we have somewhere else to go once we've consumed it. We don't. Unfortunately, earth is showing the deeply set wrinkles of our ignorance. We, and generations to come, have to live with the decisions we make today.

Within this world exists an amazing amount of wonder and goodness. From its breathtaking magnificence to the miracle of life, everything is designed to be shared, enjoyed, respected, and valued. Embrace these things in your own life. Hold them closely. Protect them.

We're all good by design. We're also very different by design – and for good reason. It's a truly brilliant feature of humanity that should be embraced and not used as a reason to separate ourselves from others who are different from us. Our differences provide much-needed balance for society and culture.

Each of us is perfect, beautiful, and yet flawed in so many extraordinarily wondrous ways. This is what defines us and makes us unique. Live life on your own terms and discover the true happiness that exists within both the world and yourself. Most importantly, remember this paragraph every time you see someone simply living, or struggling to live their life – and embrace them, their differences, and the journey they're on. This just might be their last day – and perhaps yours.

The world is a much more amazing place with you in it.
Live your life amazingly, my friend!

Fin.

Learning More...

If you would like to learn more, explore engaging video insights, and discover individualized programs that can help you discover a more remarkable life with expert guidance and assistance, please visit us today at ***IanBreck.com***.

Notes

NOTES

Notes

Notes

Notes

About the Author...

As a pioneering innovator in knowledge engineering, life and life quality research, Ian Breck is defined by an exceptional career that has been both ground breaking and inspirational. As director of knowledge research programs at Aegiss and River Bend Research, Ian has developed bodies of knowledge, expertise, and research used by some of the world's leading organizations.

Today, Ian enjoys a very different role as he focuses his energies on getting his message out that understanding life, and becoming creative with it are essential elements of living a meaningful and happy life.

Ian works with private clients to teach, mentor, and inspire them to learn more about their lives and to become creative with them in amazing new ways. In addition to his private efforts, Ian speaks, lectures, and conducts life design workshops throughout America.

Ian has lived in New York, San Francisco, Seattle, and now calls Indianapolis home.

Questions, Answers & Assistance

If you have simple questions, or would like to explore weekly issues, please feel free to visit the blog at IanBreck.com.

If you would like to work with a professional to reimagine your life in a customized and private environment, visit us online at IanBreck.com and learn about our Private Client programs or to contact us to explore the possibilities.

www.ingramcontent.com/pod-product-compliance
Lightning Source LLC
Chambersburg PA
CBHW031432160426
43195CB00010BB/697